FOUNDATIONS OF PROPHETIC MATURITY

by

Bishop R. S. Walker, I

Printed in the United States of America

Published by Bishop RS Walker Ministries formerly Another
Touch of Glory Press

2760 Crain Highway
Waldorf, Maryland 20601
Voice (301-843-9267) or (877-200-8967)
Fax (240-585-7093)
Web address: http://www.bishoprswalker.com
E-mail: admin@bishoprswalker.com

Unless otherwise quoted, scripture quotations are from the
King James Version of the Bible.

Some scripture quotations taken from KING JAMES,
Copyright@ 1954, 1958, 1962, 1964, 1965, 1987 by The
Lockman Foundation. All rights reserved. Used by
permission. (www.Lockman.org)

Some scripture quotations are taken from the Holy Bible,
New International Version®. Copyright ©1973, 1978, 1984
by International Bible Society. Used by permission of
Zondervan. All rights reserved.

ISBN: 978-0692423134 (Bishop R S Walker Ministries)

FOREWORD

This book *Foundations of Prophetic Maturity* is geared toward beginners as well as the mature believer. It was birthed out of a need a Bishop from Rocky Mount, North Carolina had with his congregation. He asked if I could prepare material that would bring his Church from basic prophetic information to a more advanced stage where they would flow in the prophetic. My team and I eagerly set out to accomplish just that. It was at a time that God started to deal with me about *Foundations of Prophetic Maturity*.

When we think about maturing any Body of people, it is necessary to start with six Blocks for building:

Building their Pool of Information

Learning outside of traditional realms of information

Observing what is not taught in verbal forms

Creating chemistry between you and your Spiritual Father/Mentor

Knowing beyond what is seen in the sense realm

Systems and principles that change facts

Our objective is to cause every person that reads this book to mature and move in their prescribed realms of the prophetic.

There are four realms of the prophetic: Basic Prophetic, Prophetic Gifting, Prophetic Ministry and the Office of the Prophet. We find that many people that feel they move in the prophetic are by no means moving at the level that God has prescribed for them. It is my desire, as Senior Prophet, to take every student and reader to the heights of understanding that God will permit and they have persistence to endure.

So why do we call this book _Foundations of Prophetic Maturity_ (plural)? _Foundations of Prophetic Maturity_ is so named because there are twelve foundations to the prophetic as there are twelve foundations to the Kingdom of God as described in the book of Revelation 21: 19-21. Some people accomplish the first foundation, but fail at other prophetic foundations. It is my desire "that you come short in no good gift" that God has for you (Ref: I Corinthians 1:7-8).

There are many people that understand there is more to this season than what they have reached up to this point. Likewise, I understand not only that there is more but, in addition, we have not scraped the barrel on what God has desired to release to us. God consistently deals with me regarding new items we could teach and write about that we'll release in the sequel to this book, _The Twelve Foundations of Prophets_. God's hand is upon you and me in this season to accomplish some amazing things, therefore, we have to pay the price for this next level of glory.

Recognition of Contributions

Acknowledgements

Thank You...To my son, Rodrick Walker, for your contribution in developing the Book Cover. To Elder Valerie Rodgers, for your contribution with formatting and organizing. To Elder Moira Washington and Elder-Elect Carla Aultmon, for your contributions with editing. To Elder Kelly Putman, Carlyn Walker and Elder Cynthia V. White for your support and assistance in preparing the book for publication. I appreciate your willingness to meet the challenges necessary to prepare this product for printing and distribution. To my son, Rodney S. Walker, Jr., Pastor Cathleen D. Moore and our entire hardworking team of Prophetic Presbyters for all of their contributions on this project. Thank you to all of my students at Bishop R. S. Walker Ministries School of the Prophets for the great questions and demand you cultivate which assist in developing me as a Prophet. Your ideas and suggestions contributed immensely to the success of this project. It is good to have all of you as part of the team. I am confident that good things will come from our joint efforts. There is no way I could get this project completed by my efforts alone. Thank you, again, for a job well done.

Dedication

This book is dedicated to my lovely wife Pastor Betty A. Walker. She has been an extraordinary blessing to me and provides tremendous support with all of my writing projects. Her encouragement and assistance, in every area of preparation, is greatly appreciated. Thank you Betty! I could not do this without you.

Table of Contents

Chapter 1

Prophetic 101

P rophetic 101 is learning how to serve well under a senior leader. This is the place where your loyalty is tried, your serving is tried and your level of communication and ability to follow instructions well is also tried because you are not moving under your own authority, name or ministry. You are moving under everything the man of God was and is.

If Elijah needed anything to happen or had particular assignments to be executed, he always involved the Prophet that was budding. (i.e. Elisha, Gehazi, Joshua, Peter). They were given particular assignments and were moving under the unction of the Prophet's words. They were not moving under their own authority, name or ministry; they were moving under everything the Man of God was.

Let's deal with the assignments of the budding Prophet because that is who is in "Prophetic 101". One of the greatest examples of a budding prophet is Elisha.

We can clearly see the assignment given to Elisha when God instructed Elijah to go and anoint him to take his place.

There were three things Elisha had to do that preceded his doing anything that Elijah would have him to do. According to **1 Kings 19:9-21**, He...

- Left the oxen/assignment.
- Kissed his biological father/got released from.
- Pursued Elijah/ran after.

One of the first assignments given to Elisha was to carry the Mantle of Elijah. Let's not make that assignment too spiritual because it just meant that he would be the one that will take care of his Spiritual father's vestments and tools for ministry.

Many that serve in the capacity of Armor Bearer or Adjutant start to feel as if they are not being used at the level of their gifting. Remember, this is "Prophetic 101" and in Prophetic 101 your gift is not fully developed and/or it is not your time to shine. The gift of the prophet is powered by his ability to be loyal to authority and serve well. One of the greatest tests you can and will encounter is can you handle the senior leaders vestments and tools for ministry well before you get yours?

We have to understand God could not use Joshua if he couldn't summit to Moses or Jesus if he couldn't submit under the hand of John **(Matthew 3:13-17)**. Likewise, Elisha would have never received vestments of his own if he couldn't master taking care of the vestments of his leader.

Responsibility To The One You Are Called To:

Let's look at the responsibility that was put on the ones that serve the Senior Leader.

> **Carry His Mantle (1 Kings 19:19b):** This assignment is not really about carrying the books and bible of the senior leader/prophet, though there is nothing wrong with that. This is really about developing a servant's heart in the Budding Prophet. There are certain things that happen when you serve at this level.
>
> **Be Ready To Follow When He Moves (1 Kings 19:20):** I have seen too many times when the Senior Leader/Prophet had to wait on the one called to serve him because he/she was not ready to serve. There are many reasons why the budding prophet called to serve is not ready. If you notice, Elisha has to go back and prepare the heart of those he was leaving

for his departure. Elisha says to Elijah, **".....and *then* I will follow thee."** Those words are an indication of someone that is asking their leader to wait on them to be ready. When the senior leader is getting ready to make an altar call, you should be ready to step in position without being called. When your senior leader is preparing to go on a ministry trip to speak, do you ask him if his vestments, car or whatever ministry tools he is using are ready or do you just notice they are not and get them ready?

Become His Servant (1 Kings 19:21): The budding prophet and the adjutant's position is one and the same particularly if that adjutant has the call to the Office of the Prophet. Both of them are recognized as the servant to the senior leader/prophet. How do you serve? There are several things we should do for those we serve and one of the benefits for doing those things is we will catch things that have not taught. The multitudes are taught, but there is not much they have not caught because they don't get close enough to their senior leader through serving. Only those who serve closely get to catch things that come out of his/her belly resulting from their intimate relationship with God.

Overcome Challenging Areas for the Budding Prophet: (2 Kings 2)

Overcoming challenging areas of the prophet's life will determine if they are ready to be released into higher places of responsibility. Your functioning as a budding prophet like Gehazi will hinder the process as a prophet. Mishandling your leader's words, name and/or dishonoring his authority would mean you could never step up and handle your leader's mantle. The one that serves well will wear the mantle well. Gehazi forfeited his position as the next senior prophet by mishandling his leader.

Be Tested on Your Ability To Stay The Course:

Prophets are spontaneous people and therefore, must stand the test of being consistent. Jesus said to the disciples, **"if you continue in my word, then are you my disciples indeed; And ye shall know the truth, and the truth shall make you free." John 8:31** It is only after you continue that you reach the status of true discipleship. Prophets that are ready for release have no problem with staying the course; being consistent with process. Elijah had to go through four seasons and Elisha had to endure those seasons with Elijah, his Spiritual father. The four seasons are: (1) Gilgal, (2) Bethel, (3) Jericho and (4) Jordan.

Have Understanding of Times (2 Kings 2:3): There were other prophetic words Elisha would hear, but he had to know when it was time for it come to pass and not just the season. Everyone else knows the season, but Elisha knew the time. The words from the other sons of the prophets were accurate, but not in time. Elisha had to understand timing as the Spiritual father knew it. This is where real sons feel the heartbeat of the father in regards to seasons and time.

See Yourself Having What's on Your Leader and Qualifying for It (2 Kings 2:9): In the midst of the Jordan Elisha asked for double of what was on Elijah. What that meant is he had to be prepared to go through what Elijah went through.

Be Able to Look Your Leader Eye to Eye (2 Kings 2:10): What does it mean to "see me"? You have to see him eye to eye, stand at his level and be able to go through what the leader went through and goes through.

Review Questions:

1. Explain the three things Elisha had to do before he could go and serve Elijah.
   * Get released from his father
   * Get Elijah approve
   * kelt the oxen

2. How is the gift of the Prophet powered? be
   By his/her ability to be loyal to authority and serve well

3. Describe not less than three areas of responsibility required in serving your senior leader. Those who serve
   1) Become his servant - will be able to get
   2) Have understanding of alot of things times - learn when and where
   3) #2 move when he moves

4. What is a determining factor in a budding prophet being ready for greater levels of responsibility?
   If they are consisted

5. A prophetic word revealed in season can still fail. Please explain why.
   you have to know the time in the season to tell

The Development of the Prophet

Chapter 2

The Undeveloped, Underdeveloped, and Developed Prophet

In case you haven't noticed yet, God places pressure on you to provoke you to produce at your maximum—even when you don't know what your maximum is. For this reason, prophets go through tremendous trials. God has to press out of them the oil that they never knew existed inside of them. There are levels of the prophet and of the prophet type that must "ooze" out of your pores. The only way this will take place is if God places a level of pressure upon you and allows you to go through things that will begin to develop you in particular areas.

As we discuss the undeveloped, underdeveloped, and developed prophet, we will find that we have existed for far too long in the place of the undeveloped or underdeveloped prophet. In fact, most people within the body of Christ — have made it all right for us to operate as undeveloped or underdeveloped prophets and live as if we were developed prophets. We have now reached a point, where God is placing pressure on us to cease from operating as undeveloped and underdeveloped prophets. We must now be willing to receive the instruction and training that will cause us to operate at our maximum and to become the developed prophet whom God desires.

The **undeveloped prophet** is a prophet who has not been developed to any level or degree. The **underdeveloped prophet** is a prophet who has been partially developed and has experienced just enough growth to fool some folks. And last, the **developed prophet** is a prophet who has withstood training, tests, trials, and temptations and, as a result, has been released into the prophetic office. This prophet is ready for "frontline" battle.

Why do most of us exist as undeveloped or underdeveloped prophets? It is because most of us refuse to be hidden. Even though you may have some clue that you're a prophet, God still wants to hide you. He doesn't want you to put "prophet" on your business cards or to place your "prophet" plaque on the outside of your office door. He doesn't want you to tell anyone.

God wants to hide you so that He can work on you. You must welcome this fact while He develops you. If we look at the life of Jesus, we find a powerful principle that teaches the importance of remaining hidden. There was a particular period in Jesus' life when people would stumble upon who Jesus was and He would direct them not to tell anyone. What would they do? They would go and tell it. Anytime they told someone who Jesus was, He had to leave the city. Jesus had to make sure that He remained hidden until His time to be revealed came.

When you get to the place where you are in hiding and you know that you're in hiding, it is then that God is able to work on you without interruption. It doesn't take as long at this point. The reason most of us are either undeveloped or underdeveloped is that whenever God is able to get us to a position where He can work on us and where He can put pressure on us, we move. In other words, we try to tell someone who we are. They in turn try to pull on us and we end up being pulled out of position. The objective is to stay in hiding long enough for God to work on us.

When we are in hiding, God works on us in various ways. Three of the things that God deals with prophets in hiding are pride, the "if you are" test, and the submission test.

Pride

Every prophet at one point or another in his or her growth will deal with the spirit of pride. It is a battle that cannot be avoided. Before prophets are developed, they must learn to recognize and defeat this spirit, lest it wreak havoc in their ministry and their lives.

The "if you are" test

Most of the time, we battle and fail this test. This test places prophets in the position where they must prove that they are really prophets. If we had remained in hiding, there would have been no need for this particular test. No one would have known that you called yourself a prophet. Therefore, the opportunity to challenge you to prove yourself as such would never have presented itself.

Submission

Most prophets fail this test several times before passing. You have to be sharp for the test of submission, so sharp that your mission gets lost in that leader's mission. It is imperative that you arrive at the point in your life where even though you realize that you have a ministry, you actually declare, like Jesus, **"My will is to do the will of him who sent me."** Then you have to

 **Key Point:**

God is the only one who can call you, but He leaves it up to man to choose you.

figure out who sent you. Did God send you, or did your man or woman of God send you?

The Bible tells us that many are called but few are chosen. **(Matthew. 20:16)** The one who chooses you is actually the one who sends you. One of the things we have to understand is that God calls you. No one else can call you. However, unless we come to the point where we have been selected and chosen; hand-picked by man, we have no right to ministry.

> *"Now after the death of Moses the servant of the LORD it came to pass, that the LORD spake unto Joshua the son of Nun, Moses' minister, saying,…"*
> *Joshua 1:1*

Wasn't Joshua God's minister? Well then, who was Moses? He was God's servant. Joshua was, as a matter of fact, Moses' minister. And Moses was the servant of the Lord. Understand that if I am the leader and you are sent to me, both of us can't be the servants of God. God is going to give direction to the one who is called, hand-picked, and anointed to serve Him.

If we go a little further into the Book of Numbers, we find God talking to Moses:

"And the LORD said unto Moses, Gather unto me seventy men of the elders of Israel, whom thou knowest to be the elders of the people, and officers over them; and bring them unto the tabernacle of the congregation, that they may stand there with thee. And I will come down and talk with thee there: and I will take of the spirit which is upon thee, and will put it upon them; and they shall bear the burden of the people with thee, that thou bear it not thyself alone." Numbers 11:16-17

Please notice that God took of **"the spirit that was upon Moses"** and placed it upon the seventy who were elders indeed. "Moses, if you have some trouble out of them, it's your own fault because you selected them. You chose them and then you sent them to do what I called you to do."

You have to know where you're assigned and to whom you're assigned. Just because you don't like the church doesn't mean you can jump up and leave. **I Corinthians 12:28** lets us know, **"And God hath set some in the church, first apostles, secondarily prophets, thirdly teachers, after that miracles, then**

gifts of healings, helps, governments, diversities of tongues." Who set them in the church? God.

If you are at a church and God leads you, you must have been sent and set by God. If you are potted in that place as a flower that is potted by God, no one should "repot" you except God. There's no "repotting" done except when the gardener, God, "repots" you. Any flower that can plant and "repot" itself is a freak of nature and of no use in the Kingdom. God will send you to a place so that you can be made, not so that you can uproot and "repot" yourself whenever you encounter something that doesn't tickle your fancy.

Wherever God sets you, you must stay put because you're going through a serious test of submission. I know, "They talk to me like a dog! They talk to me like I'm stupid or something! Submit? 'I ain't submitting to nothing!'" Well, you just failed the test.

Submission—Case in Point

Mark 7:24-29—The Syrophoenician Woman

The Syrophoenician woman went to Jesus and besought Him that He would cast the Devil out of her child. Jesus responded, **"Let the children first be filled: for it is not meet to take the children's bread, and to cast it unto the dogs."** She began her response with the following words, **"Yes Lord: yet..."** How did she address Him? She called Him "Lord" after being recognized as a dog. In essence, what she said was, "Jesus, it doesn't matter to me if I pick it up off the floor or if it's leftovers. The only thing I want is for my request to be answered." In turn, Jesus complimented her on her faith. That's all she needed to hear Him say—"You got what you asked for." Her request was filled only because she passed the submission test.

As a prophet, passing the submission test is a must. If the spirit of pride had been present in this Syrophoenician woman, she would have risen up at being compared to a dog. But, she didn't. She passed the pride test. In like manner, should your man or woman of God say something that you don't like, you need to lie down like a dog, roll over, and play dead.

 **Key Point:**

Prophets must endeavor to become developed so that the prophetic voice can be released in the earth, so that God's will, mind, and purposes might be made known.

The developed prophet has mastered this response. The undeveloped and underdeveloped prophet have yet to move into this place of maturity and humility where the spirit of pride is ruled over and not a ruler.

The Budding Prophet

Many of you may already have an idea of where you fit in the prophetic, while others may still be discovering their place within this ministry or office.

Regardless of your specific assignment, by now you must have identified if you are an undeveloped, underdeveloped, or developed prophet.

The budding prophet is a prophet who has been hand-picked for development. This prophet type has not yet reached the full stage of development, but he or she is "knee-deep" in the development process.

One of the best examples of a budding prophet lies in the story of Elijah and Elisha. When we trail the life of Elisha, we will learn that Elisha was found walking behind oxen and not in a tent passing out his business cards. He was called as a prophet, but he was not fulfilling any portion of the prophetic. As a budding prophet, it is important to know where you fit within the scope of the prophetic.

As we deal with **1 Kings 19**, we will explore the situation that surrounded Elijah's life and what Elisha was walking into. This is the part of the prophetic that we don't understand. When you hook up with your man or woman of God, you were walking into something. Whether you understood or not what was actually taking place is irrelevant; the fact remained that you indeed walked into something when you made the connection. God, on the other hand, understood everything. He knew exactly what you were walking into and knew that what you were walking into would be for your development.

Most of us are familiar with the life of Elijah and with both his victories and defeats. We love to recall his victories, but we must realize that amongst his many successes, Elijah had particular issues. If we revisit his life, we will remember that one of his issues came with the name "Jezebel" written on it. Jezebel had it out for Elijah. Elijah, at this juncture in his life, had encountered victory on the mount where he literally called down fire. He called down fire and then ran from a woman called Jezebel. Anytime prophets meet up with trouble, they run into their caves.

"And he came thither unto a cave, and lodged there; and, behold, the word of the LORD came to him, and he said unto him, What doest thou here, Elijah?" 1 Kings 19:9

Elijah, in a time of trouble, ran to a cave and lodged there. He wasn't thinking about coming out of that cave. But, the Bible says that the Word of the Lord came to him even when he was in the cave.

When you run to your respective caves, do not expect to get another Word from God. Once in your cave, will you receive the Word that comes to you? Listen. You will get the same Word in your cave that Elijah received; "What are you doing here?"

After all that you've gone through, after all of the things that God delivered you from, after receiving forgiveness for the things you've done, after surviving all of the things that people did to you, what could you possibly be doing in the cave? God just doesn't understand. God looks at the deposit that He placed inside of you, and for that reason He doesn't understand why you're in the cave.

Often times we try to get away so that we can hear God. But, how many times do we have to run away to hear Him? God needs a prophet who can go through the battle and still hear Him. He needs us to be able to be in the midst of a storm and to say, "Peace be still" and still be able to hear Him. Then, the storm can resume.

 Key Point:

A sabbatical is not undertaken so that you can hear God. A sabbatical is intended for you to get yourself together.

Be aware of the fact that you are in control of the stuff around you — the stuff around you is not in control of you. You cannot, however, tell the stuff around you to be still because it has a purpose. It has to fulfill its course, but it must not be permitted to interrupt what God is saying to you.

In **1 Kings 19:10**, Elijah declares his jealousy for the Lord.

> *"And he said, I have been very jealous for the LORD*

God of hosts: for the children of Israel have forsaken thy covenant, thrown down thine altars, and slain thy prophets with the sword; and I, even I only, am left; and they seek my life, to take it away."

In other words, Elijah said, "I'm jealous. They forsook your covenant and threw down your altars and have slain your prophets with the sword, and I'm the only one that's left who's been doing it right. I can't figure out, God, why won't you do something about this woman who is after me and is seeking to take my life!" As prophets, a lot of times we feel as if we're doing something that no one else is doing and we can't figure out why we were dealt such a bitter hand.

In the following verses, **1 Kings 19:11-12**, God told Elijah to leave the cave:

"And he said, Go forth, and stand upon the mount before the LORD. And, behold, the LORD passed by, and a great and strong wind rent the mountains, and brake in pieces the rocks before the LORD; but

the LORD was not in the wind: and after the wind an earthquake; but the LORD was not in the earthquake: And after the earthquake a fire; but the LORD was not in the fire: and after the fire a still small voice."

What does your cave look like? Let's not just think of the cave as some place that we retreat to from life's storms. When you didn't want anything else to do with another man, you retreated to a cave. What cave? The cave of "no-man." You retreated to a place where you would never encounter another man. The same holds true for the man who wanted nothing else to do with a woman. When you became fed up with or hurt by leadership, you retreated to a cave. What cave? The cave of "leaders with no leadership ability." Many times when we are in this situation, we will search out and connect with a leader who really has no leadership ability to avoid the potential of being hurt again. Retreating is not the answer. As God told Elijah, I must tell you, "Go forth and stand."

The command to go forth and stand is very important to the life of the budding prophet. Before God allowed the wind to come, He told Elijah to do two things: Go forth and stand. The budding prophet has to be willing to be taught how to do these two things.

As we considered **1 Kings 19:11-12**, we saw that God was not in the earthquake, the great wind, or the fire. He was in the still, small voice. We should never be led by the results of the great wind, earthquake, or fire. Often we refuse to go forth and stand because our focus is placed on the earthquake, the wind, or the fire instead of going forth and standing.

"And he said, I have been very jealous for the LORD God of hosts: because the children of Israel have forsaken thy covenant, thrown down thine altars, and slain thy prophets with the sword; and I, even I only, am left; and they seek my life, to take it away. And the LORD said unto him, Go, return on thy way to the wilderness of Damascus: and when thou comest, anoint Hazael to be king over Syria: And Jehu the son of Nimshi shalt thou anoint to be king over Israel: and Elisha the son of Shaphat of Abelmeholah shalt thou anoint to be prophet in thy room. And it shall come to pass, that him that escapeth the sword of Hazael shall Jehu slay: and him that escapeth from the sword of Jehu shall Elisha slay. Yet I have left me seven thousand in Israel, all the

knees which have not bowed unto
Baal, and every mouth which hath not
kissed him. So he departed thence,
and found Elisha the son of Shaphat,
who was plowing with twelve yoke of
oxen before him, and he with twelfth:
and Elijah passed by him, and cast his
mantle upon him."
1 Kings 19:14-19

In verse 14, the "I" syndrome makes an appearance. Notice how many times Elijah uses the word "I." His use of this word is a clear indication that he is still concerned that the folks did not measure up to how he was walking.

In verse 15, God tells Elijah to return to the wilderness, but this time his return to the wilderness will bring him into contact with someone. This time his trip through the wilderness is to anoint someone. And last but not least, "Elijah, why don't we just go ahead and replace you. Elijah, I realize that you're stressed out, but you are coming very close to becoming self-righteous, yet, you still have your mind on Me. Because of your purpose, Elijah, I can't allow you to become this self-righteous man. I must get you out of this. I must replace you before you become this person. Yes, you are anointed, but I cannot permit self-righteousness to dwell and mature in you."

Now enters Elisha. What in the world could Elisha possibly gain from a man like Elijah? What could he possibly want from such a man? Why would he want to follow a man who had so many issues? To Elisha, none of these things mattered. He was ready to bud as a prophet and willing to do what it took to get himself there. He wasn't interested in how Elijah failed but in how he overcame his failures.

In verse 19, we see that the mantle was shifted. Elijah had to have a successor. At this point, he was more conscious of succession than he was of selfishness. He understood that Elisha was who he was since God had already preordained him to be the prophet in his room or to be his successor. When a successor is selected, the demon of jealousy raises its ugly head.

We learned that there were seven thousand who had not bowed the knee to or kissed Baal, yet Elisha was chosen as the successor. God picked a boy who was walking behind oxen and who was loyal to his biological father and overlooked the seven thousand previously mentioned. That's enough to provoke jealousy in anyone's heart! As a matter of fact, many of us would have been offended by this selection. But, how could we have been? We didn't know that person's story.

What exactly was Elisha's story? Well, he was plowing behind twelve oxen and tending to his father's business. HE WAS WORKING. God provides for people who are working. Do you realize how many people want to be married? They will uproot all of the men or women who are hanging out and will attend the church that has the most available men or women. They become watchers and never really get anyone. If God is to present them, they must work. Likewise, if you're looking for the anointing to descend upon you, stop looking. God will not place the anointing on you simply because you're chasing it. He will place the anointing upon you when you become very conscious of your man or woman of God's assignment and less conscious of your own assignment. Most of us, however, are still chasing the anointing and have yet to apprehend it.

Elisha didn't chase the anointing or the mantle. It was cast upon him. This investiture, in simple terms said, "Follow me." You can't just cast your anointed mantle upon just anyone. You have to make sure that people have "staying power." You can't just tell anyone to follow you or beg anyone to follow you, either. Elijah said it one time only, and he didn't actually *say* it. Elisha, however, knew exactly what the casting of the mantle meant. He knew that he was budding and made the proper arrangements to follow Elijah.

Elisha's response to receiving Elijah's mantle shows his deep sense of loyalty. The boy had himself together! Elisha agreed to follow Elijah but first had to bid his parents goodbye. He requested that he be allowed to go and kiss his father and mother, and after doing so, left that assignment to follow Elijah. He acknowledged the shifting of the mantle and his own willingness to follow

Elijah, but managed to stay in order and obtain a release from his parents first.

In addition, prior to leaving his parents Elisha offered a sacrifice. He was in order. He was ready to bud as a prophet. How many of you feel that you are ready to bud as a prophet? Well, what does your tithing record look like? Do you even tithe? What about sacrificial giving?

After Elisha made the proper arrangements, he arose and went after Elijah to serve and minister to him. He became Elijah's minister. The Bible didn't acknowledge him as a minister of God, but as Elijah's minister; Elisha served a man. This serving prepared him for budding. Until budding prophets learn that they must serve the person to whom they are submitted, they will always remain in a stage of "un-development" or "underdevelopment."

In **2 Kings 2,** we observe how Elisha endured everything that his man of God, Elijah, endured. His perseverance entitled him to the anointing that was on the prophet Elijah and to the anointing that Elijah stood in line to receive. "What if my man of God does not live out his full course?" If you serve your man of God and he leaves this life early, you are entitled to the anointing that was on him at the time of his departure and to the anointing that never came to him.

Your heart of service toward the man of God determines the level of anointing that you are entitled to. Please notice the definitive article, "**the**." Someone is responsible for making sure that the correct endowment comes upon you.

That place is found as you submit to your man or woman of God. Budding prophets, if they are to effectively bud into developed prophets, must realize this and seek to submit themselves so that they might be what they were created to be.

Review Questions:

1. What are the behaviors of an undeveloped prophet?

2. What are the characteristics of a developed prophet?

3. How does the undeveloped prophet differ from the underdeveloped prophet?

4. Describe how the spirit of pride hinders a budding from coming into maturity?

5. What is a budding prophet?

Anointing – Hidden in the House

Chapter 3

There is a time period that hides you as a prophet in order for you to mature. **In that place you are <u>protected</u>, <u>nurtured</u>, <u>shaped and</u> <u>fine tuned</u>.** During this time of hiding, the anointing is poured on you before your season changes and you shift into that season to be manifested. **Once your season changes, Satan has a right to try and attack you to see if he can turn you around.**

Hidden From the Anointing Killer

We have entered a season where there is an assault on the anointing on the body of Christ. We have also entered a season where there is an assault on the anointing on our lives. We have shifted to a new place and there is an anointing on the life of each and every one of us that we must protect with everything that we have. The anointing that is on your life is under attack and you must do what you are supposed to do in order to guard your anointing and protect it.

"And when Athaliah the mother of Ahaziah saw that her son was dead, she arose and destroyed all the seed royal. But Jehosheba, the daughter of king Joram, sister of Ahaziah, took Joash the son of Ahaziah, and stole him from among the king's sons which were slain; and they hid him, even him and his nurse, in the bedchamber from Athaliah, so that he was not slain. And he was with her hid in the house of the LORD six years. And Athaliah did reign over the land." 2 Kings 11:1-3

The anointing that is on your life is on you for a specific reason. Too many of us have been so accustomed to doing church as usual that we are not really clear that there is anointing on us. There is anointing in us and on us. The anointing that is in you is in you for good and for a very specific reason. It is in you so that you will be able to come to the highest height in God that your flesh will allow. Most people in the body of Christ never reach the height of their anointing because their flesh has prevented them from doing that. It is not that God did not want us to reach the highest height; it is that our flesh has prevented us from going there. There is an anointing that is upon you and that anointing seems to shift. That anointing is on one assignment in this season, but the next season it shifts to another assignment.

There is a reason why the anointing is on us in this particular season. The enemy cannot see what is in you, but he can see what is on you. When he gets a whiff of what is on your life, he comes after what's on you.

There is a link between what your assignment is and the anointing you pay, that rests on you. One of the problems is that most of us are not really willing to pay for the anointing that is on us. This means is that you cannot go where you want to go, you cannot do what you want to do and you cannot pursue what you think you need to be pursuing.

It is called Athaliah

Athaliah was the daughter of Ahab and had become a queen after her mother Jezebel. However, the spirit of Athaliah is an anointing killer. Her objective once her son died was to go after all of the king's seed and to make sure that she was in power. Too much attention is given to those that would tell you that if you are a woman and because you wear makeup, you have a Jezebel spirit. If we could get the church world that is a voice in front of the people off by thinking that the spirit of Jezebel had to do with makeup, when Jezebel really comes after you, you won't recognize it. The spirit of Jezebel really does live and it has had her name changed. That name is Athaliah, an anointing killer.

The spirit of Jezebel will go after that which the anointing is passed on to. One way to identify it is that it is perverted. It takes a certain kind of perversion for a grandmother to kill her own seed in order to take office. She was killing all of her son's children so that they would not come into power so that she would reign. But her sister took the youngest son, Joash, into the bedchamber of the Lord and hid him for six years. Even though he was a baby at that time, there was an anointing on him. The objective was to guard the anointing on Joash because he was the king. There was an anointing in him and on him because he was to step into office and carry out a particular assignment.

 **Key Point:**

God has already ordained and set you aside for a very specific reason so that you would step into power. The spirit of Jezebel goes after the authority.

This was the first time a woman ever stepped into office as a Queen. And it was because she wiped out all of the king's sons. It is because she wiped out all of the authority. The job of Athaliah is to make sure that you who are supposed to step into power, never get at the gate of power because we do not protect what is in us nor do we protect what is on us.

Now there are a lot of us that are power seekers - we are seeking something. We want to be great, rather than just operating on the anointing that lives in us right now. We want to rush this thing and we want to become somebody. But God says just stay with the anointing that is on us. Do not seek opportunity or fame; just stay with the anointing that is on you for now. The fact that we may be chasing fame means that we are already following something. That something we are already following is Athaliah and it is set out to kill the anointing that is on you.

Athaliah and Spiritual Authority

What saved Joash was the fact that he was hidden in the bedchamber of the Lord. Athaliah was not interested in the bedchamber of the Lord. She was not interested in the house of the Lord. When it comes down to that spirit, there is a disinterest in authority. When God sets up spiritual authority, it is for our protection.

Spiritual authority will take us into the bedchamber. Athaliah is a whore spirit; it is a spirit of prostitution and it does not want to make a commitment. When it comes down to being a wife, she has signed on the dotted line saying; "I am with you for the rest of my time. I am committed to you and I am submitted to you. You are my man and I am your wife." We are talking about covenant and commitment, but we are also talking about the church.

Have you ever heard someone say that they are only at a particular church for a season? That is the spirit of Athaliah. You should be committed to whatever you marry. Whenever you come into a covenant with something, you should be committed. The spirit of Athaliah does not want to be seen with you and she knows that you don't want to be seen with her. She will do whatever she needs to do to make sure that she is pumped out at the top, pumped out in the back and make sure that her legs are looking good and smelling sweet just so that she can lie with you. But a wife is different because she wants a commitment; a whore does not. So God is saying, protect the anointing on your life. In this entire prophetic realm there is a need to rise up in a commitment. There is a need for us to rise up and say, God I am committed to you. Whatever you say is what I want. I don't have my own will anymore because I want you."

"But Jehosheba, the daughter of king Joram, sister of Ahaziah, took Joash the son of Ahaziah and stole him from among the king's sons which were slain; and they hid him, even him and his nurse, in the bedchamber from Athaliah, so that he was not slain." 2 Kings 11:2

God sees what you are to become and He has put something on the inside of you that He is not going to let a whore get to. God is not going to let anything take you down so He had you stolen from where you were and had you hidden in the house. God has to come after you and grab you from where you were and hide you in the house. If we are not careful after having escaped the spirit of Athaliah, the spirit may reattach itself to us.

Instead of us abiding in the bedchamber the Lord, we start to run out of the bedchamber allowing Athaliah to see us and recognize that we are the anointed of the Lord and get her next opportunity to kill us.

The enemy comes after you because of the anointing and he is the Athaliah that wants to kill the anointing that is on you. When you and I run all over the place and run where we want to go, we are opening ourselves up to the spirit of Athaliah and it has an assignment against your anointing.

The Important Reason for a Covering

There is a rising up from where we are and we have to rise up because we know that we are not protected. That is the important reason for a covering. You have to make sure that you are under the cover. You have to also make sure that the covering that you are under is strong enough to hold you.

Rebellion

Rebellion is at the root of Athaliah; not just rebellion but corruption and perversion lives in her roots. Once you allow Athaliah to get her hook into you, your spirit starts to change. In **Luke 4:18-21** Jesus said, **"The Spirit of the Lord is upon me, because he hath anointed me to preach the gospel to the poor; he hath sent me to heal the brokenhearted, to preach deliverance to the captives, and recovering of sight to the blind, to set at liberty them that are bruised, To preach the acceptable year of the Lord. And he**

closed the book, and he gave *it* again to the minister, and sat down. And the eyes of all them that were in the synagogue were fastened on him. And he began to say unto them, This day is this scripture fulfilled in your ears."

If you notice in this passage, Jesus went through the whole thing that He was assigned to do and after that He began to say something, but they would not let Him finish talking. They said in **Luke 4:22, "And they said, Is not this Joseph's son?"** They wanted to kill His anointing. Why? Because the anointing rose up and when His anointing was seen, there was the spirit of Athaliah that wanted to kill it in the house of God. Remember when your anointing is seen, Athaliah comes after it to kill it.

 **Key Point:**

Athaliah wants to become intimate with you and then does not want you to tell anybody.

There is safety in the bedchamber. If you are challenged in your prayer life, it means that Athaliah is trying to pull you out of the bedchamber because in the bedchamber is where you are intimate with God. Remember, your *wife* is in the bedchamber. You never take a whore into the bedchamber. Another thing about a wife is that you do not keep secrets from her. When you are intimate with your wife, you do not have secrets from your wife.

Another way to identify Athaliah is that she wants you to keep secrets from the father or who God has set over your life that is designed to protect you. Athaliah is male or female. When it comes down to sons of God, they are male or female. When it comes down to the bride of Christ, they are male or female. When it comes down to spiritual fathers, they are male or female. When it comes down to the spirit of Jezebel, it is male or female and when it comes down to the spirit of Korah, it is male or female.

You have to stay hidden in the house until it is time for your anointing to be exposed. The reason you are hidden in the house is so that your anointing would grow. It will grow strong and by the time your anointing is six years old, you are ready to be exposed. Joash was hidden in the house for six years. He was seven years old when he was crowned king. He was not crowned until he was complete. It is not time to come out of the house until you are complete.

There is an anointing that is on your life even if it does not seem that one is there. In the bedchamber is where we get that anointing developed. In the bedchamber, we can prophecy and be wrong; and no one will call us a false prophet. We can get corrected in the bedchamber as long as we are submitted under authority. We can get cleaned up in the bedchamber. But once we come out of the bedchamber and we miss it, they will assassinate us. When we come out of the bedchamber and we prophecy wrong, they will crucify us.

Those of you that are getting married have to make sure that you are not marrying Athaliah. Whether male or female, if you marry the spirit of Athaliah, it is going to be rough. Remember, the one thing that Athaliah does is to seek opportunity to come into the place where you really live and assassinate your anointing.

 **Review Questions:**

1. What transpires in the life of prophets while they are hidden?

2. What are the three spirits rooted in Athaliah?

3. Who is Athaliah?

4. What are some of the ways to identify the spirit of Athaliah in operation?

5. What is the difference in the anointing being in you and upon you?

Understanding Mandated Authority

Chapter 4

(Local, Regional and National)

I n this lesson you learn a about the call of the prophet and the authority that each one walks in as handed down by God. Every prophet will fit in one category or the other. There is regional, local, national and international authority. A prophet must understand how to walk in each one because operating in the right office with the wrong authority could be quite chaotic for the prophet and for the jurisdiction he or she serves.

Authority, Order and Structure

God wants prophetic people and prophets to bring authority, order, and structure. When God sends you into a situation, it is going to be void and without form.

God wants us to change things the way He did in **Genesis 1:3. "And God said, Let there be light, and there was light."** Light came by His saying; and that is what we must do. We must speak to things, situations, circumstances and etcetera. When God asks us to carry out a particular assignment, we do not want to do it because of the way the people act.

God sends us in at the beginning of something so that we can bring form and order to those particular situations. Many of us tell God that we are not able to bring order and structure because we need that in our own lives, but we become first partakers when set ourselves in order by speaking the words that bring order to our lives.

For example, if you are a person who bounces checks, then speak to that situation and say that you are not going to do that anymore and change some things. Another example is that of a single man looking for a wife. God is not necessarily going to send you a person exactly according to what you have in your mind; therefore, you must speak to what you desire and keep on saying that. We must stop *verbalizing* what we see and start *declaring* what God says about it! Use all of the power and authority in your office to bring about change in your area of authority.

Matthew 16:18: ". . . upon this Rock I will build my church . . ." was Jesus' prophetic proclamation of the New Testament church. Jesus preached, taught and demonstrated the power of the Gospel of the Kingdom of God as portrayed by Matthew. He presented the spiritual and heavenly kingdom that could only be entered into by repentance and faith. The Kingdom of God was given to a nation that would bring forth the fruits thereof, thus the background is set for the building of His church.

Ephesians 4 depicts the gifts given by Jesus. It is through these gifts that Jesus establishes the structure of church leadership. Ephesians 4 also gives an exhortation of the privileges and responsibilities of the Christian through unity and love. It also includes an explanation of how "the body" would be led and the means by which it would function and mature.

Properly termed the "ascension gifts" (ministry), they are commonly referred to as the "five-fold ministry." The foundational purposes for these gifts are also described in **Ephesians 4:12-13 "For the perfecting of the saints, for the work of the ministry, for the edifying of the body of Christ: Till we all come in the unity of the faith, and of the knowledge of the Son of God, unto a perfect man, unto the measure of the stature of the fulness of Christ:"**

The Apostle Paul prophetically reveals in **Ephesians 4:8** that everything the body of Christ would need to grow and mature was established by Jesus: "**....When he ascended up on high, he led captivity captive, and he gave gifts unto men.**" As we specifically examine the gift of the prophet, we will identify his purpose, responsibilities, and the duration that he will exist in the church.

The "ascension gifts" brought authority, order, and structure to the church. The Apostle Paul further depicts the ranking responsibility in the order of the apostle, prophet, evangelist, pastor and teacher. **"And he gave some, apostles; and some prophets; and some, evangelists; and some pastors and teachers." Ephesians 4:11**

Regional Information Should Be Available to Prophets

When something happens in your region, you should know about it! Nothing should happen in your region without your knowledge. When something happens in your family, you should know about it. An amazing revelation of this knowledge is seen in **2 Kings 4:28, "Then she said, Did I desire a son of my lord? did I not say, Do not deceive me?"** She was expecting her son to live. So what did the prophet do? He raised him from the dead.

We must have an ear to the mouth of God because there are particular things that God is going to reveal to us in this our time. We are going to have to be sensitive to what God is saying and make sure that we are running after God with everything that we have.

Prophetic Order

One of the places prophetic people are greatly challenged is in the area of prophetic order - knowing what to do and when to do it. Operating in disorder at any level happens because of no prophetic training and disorder breeds more disorder. God expected us to ask Him when to speak, because He may not be talking about now. This kind of disorder can cause a word to be released in error or a word to be released out-of-time potentially causing chaos in the life or lives of the individuals you release it to.

The Prophet is a divine gift and is used of God as His mouthpiece. Prophets have their ears to God's mouth and the Holy Spirit is speaking to prophets, telling them what to do and when. For this reason, prophets and prophetic people are sensitive to times and seasons. You never have to worry about God telling you what is going to happen in the next season because He is always speaking. You may or may not hear Him, but He is always speaking. Nothing will happen in your house that you don't know about. The Holy Spirit will tell you prior to it happening.

If we speak what God is saying and according to His word, the Devil does not know if it is you or God talking because we are mysteriously hidden in God. So as long as you say what God is saying, the Devil does not know whether we are talking or God is talking. But **when we** *deviate from the word of God, then the Devil can see us!*

Being mysteriously hidden in God, positions us to have knowledge of visions and revelations of the Lord. **2 Corinthians 12:1-4 "It is not expedient for me doubtless to glory. I will come to visions and revelations of the Lord. I knew a man in Christ above fourteen years ago, (whether in the body, I cannot tell; or whether out of the body, I cannot tell: God knoweth;) such an one caught up to the third heaven. And I knew such a man, (whether in the body, or out of the body, I cannot tell: God knoweth;) How that he was caught up into paradise, and heard unspeakable words, which it is not lawful for a man to utter."**

Now according to this passage, Paul cannot tell if he is in his body or out of his body. This is because he is hidden in God. When you are hidden in God, you come into visions and revelations of the Lord. Sometimes when people see you operate like this, they may ask you if you are like a palm reader, psychic or diviner. Having this knowledge, vision, and revelations of the Lord is nothing like a palm readers or psychics. They are of a different spirit and cannot know anything until someone in the body of Christ speaks what the Holy Spirit has already given them.

Confidentiality

Confidentiality is also a very important part of prophetic order. Gossip is one of things that prophets are challenged with; and gossip is unauthorized information. If you operate in unauthorized information, your anointing is at stake. We are managers of words and we must be good stewards of our words. When you are confidential, God will give you information about people in order to help them. When He knows that you are not going to put their information out in the street, He knows that He can trust you with people's hearts and with people's feelings. Therefore, He will also give you unspeakable things and He will tell you some unspeakable things about people.

God wants to fellowship with you. God has some words that He needs to get out and He is looking for someone who will be able to hear Him. He is in heaven and He cannot do anything past your authority because He has given man authority over the earth. He needs you to hear it because you are your brothers' keeper. God takes you to a level where you have understanding that passes knowledge.

The Old Testament Order

The prophetic institution was not a temporary position established for superiority of position; provision was made for it in the law. The reason provision was made for it in the law was so that the Israelites might not consult with false prophets such as diviners, observers of times, and enchanters.

Diviners, observers of times, and enchanters were recognized as the pagan counterpart to the prophets of God. Diviners differ from prophets. A *"diviner"* is a human being used for unwarranted prying into the future by magical arts. The prophet is a *"divine gift"*.

The *"observer"* comes from the Greek word *"skopos."* From skopos, we get the English word *"scope,"* meaning to look or observe. *"Times"* is derived from the word *"harra"* or *"horror."* From this etymology derived the word *"horoscope."* The *"enchanter"* is one who practices exorcism. Incantations or magic ritual procedures enlist the aid of evil spirits or set free the demonized from their torments.

The scriptures do not represent an unbroken series of prophets for each was inducted into office by his predecessor; except in the cases of Joshua and Elisha, who were respectively inducted into office by Moses and Elijah. The prophets are described as deriving their prophetic office immediately from God.

Moses prophesied of **"..... a Prophet like from the midst of thee, of thy brethren, like unto me; unto him ye shall hearken; .... I will raise them up a Prophet from among their brethren, like unto thee, and will put my words in his mouth; and he shall speak unto them all that I shall command him. And** it shall come to pass, *that* whosoever will not hearken unto my words which he shall speak in my name, I will require *it* of him." **Deuteronomy 18:15, 18-19** Although this passage is considered as a reference to the Messiah, it does not exclude its reference to a succession of prophets between Moses and Christ, running parallel with the kingdom of Israel.

In the time of the Old Testament, specifically during the days from Joshua to Eli, the visions of prophecy became less frequent. During the time of the judges- the priesthood, was the original instrument through which Israel was governed and taught in spiritual things. Similar to today's religious era, the people became less sensitive and were no longer affected by the plans and order put in place by God.

Within the Levitical priesthood, God called out and raised up Samuel of the family of Kohath (**I Chronicles 6:28**), as the instrument for effecting a reform in the priestly order and giving to the prophets a position of importance that they had never before held. Samuel did not create the prophetic order as a new thing. He orchestrated the qualities of both the prophetic and regal order given in the law to the Israelites by Moses (**Deuteronomy 13:1, 18:18 and 20-22**). Again, the order or role of the prophet was not yet developed because there was not yet a demand for them.

New Testament Order

In the New Testament order of the prophetic, we see some things that will help us in the way we move throughout the local assembly. For example, we have seen people that would prophesy in testimonial services. There would be incidents where a person would prophesy in the midst of a sermon, and they would not even be the guests.

We, as prophets, **MUST** remember that God is a gentleman and will not break through to interrupt you or anyone else, not even to get His word through. God is a God of order. It is always proper order to:

1. Wait for the opening, and

2. Wait for the leading to get the word through that God has given.

You can have a genuine word from the Lord that could be rejected because of your lack of wisdom in delivering it. Don't assume that just because God said it, your message will be automatically received. Someone who wants change rarely rejects accuracy. In the mind of the prophet, any accuracy is not easily rejected because of the pressure that God puts on him when He is giving it.

The Office of the Prophet

The office of the prophet carries the authority to rebuke, correct, root out, pull down, destroy, throw down, build, and to plant. The office of the prophet also carries with it the authority to judge prophecy. The situations and circumstances that bring the prophet to judge can and should be done by the one who occupies the office. Those who fall in the other categories could possibly know some of the situations and circumstances that would come under judgment. However, they are not allowed to do anything about it. If they find themselves judging, they could be found fighting God or against the up-line.

God has privileged some to know and understand certain things. He could very well be bringing those persons into the office of the prophet. These individuals must first test their level of discipline to prove whether God can trust them.

 **Review Questions:**

1. God uses prophets and prophetic gifts to bring three things. What are they?

2. What are the three categories of false prophets and how does each category function?

3. How do diviners differ from prophets?

4. What is prophetic order?

5. Why is confidentiality an important part of prophetic order?

The Heart of the Prophet

Chapter 5

M any of us have not been introduced to the prophet's heart. It is possible to have a prophet's anointing and a prophet's call and not have a prophet's heart. We want to make sure that we are really getting what God is saying regarding the prophet's heart. We are going to see how God displays the heart of the prophet in the book of Jeremiah.

Let's begin in **Jeremiah 8:18-22:** "*When I would comfort myself against sorrow, my heart is faint in me. Behold the voice of the cry of the daughter of my people because of them that dwell in a far country: Is not the LORD in Zion? is not her king in her? Why have they provoked me to anger with their graven images, and with strange vanities? The harvest is past, the summer is ended, and we are not* *saved. For the hurt of the daughter of my people am I hurt; I am black; astonishment hath taken hold on me. Is there no balm in Gilead; is there no physician there? why then is not the health of the daughter of my people recovered?"*

As we begin to think about this portion of scripture, we are going to see God's example of the prophet's heart. One of the things we see is in verse 18, **"When I would comfort myself against sorrow; my heart is faint in me."** Jeremiah is saying that when he would comfort himself, his heart is weak. The heart of the prophet is to identify with the condition of the people. Sometimes we as prophets become insensitive to the condition of the people we must speak to or to the region we must speak into. As a result, we never speak to the situation or into the people and because of that they never really change.

Sometimes our heart becomes callous because we have shifted from the level of responsibility that God handed to us regarding our region. So as we begin to think about our respective region, nation, kingdom or wherever God has given us charge, we must determine if we have the prophet's heart in that given situation. We can determine whether we have a prophet's heart by how we speak to the situation. Whether we are speaking of a nation, a kingdom, the people in a kingdom, one group or another; however far your region reaches we must have a heart for that group and begin to speak the word of the Lord to the situation of that particular group.

Now watch what God says as we take a look at verse 19, **"Behold the voice of the cry of the daughter of my people."** The daughter of his people is crying out, but the prophets are not hearing. Can one really distinguish one cry from the other? As a prophet, if you hear somebody cry, can you make a distinction between the cries? This means that you and I are going to have to be very sensitive to the heart of God because when God hears a cry, He knows exactly what kind of a cry it is and He responds to that kind of cry. There is one cry that God expects you and me to respond to and then there is another cry that God responds to Himself, as He did with the situation of the tower of Babel. **Genesis 11:5. "And the LORD came down to see the city and the tower, which the children of men builded."**

The children of Israel cried in Egypt. The account of this can be found in **Exodus 2:23-25: "And it came to pass in process of time, that the king of Egypt died: and the children of Israel sighed by reason of the bondage, and they cried, and their cry came up unto God by reason of the bondage. And God heard their groaning, and God remembered his covenant with Abraham, with Isaac, and with Jacob. And God looked upon the children of Israel, and God had respect unto them."**

The Book of Esther provides another example. Esther's level of comfort was interrupted because of a cry that was released through Mordecai while sitting outside of the gate. God heard the cry. **Esther 4:1-2: "When Mordecai perceived all that was done, Mordecai rent his clothes, and put on sackcloth with ashes, and went out into the midst of the city, and cried with a loud and a bitter cry; And came even before the king's gate: for none *might* enter into the king's gate clothed with sackcloth."**

Now you and I as prophets and prophetic people have to identify the kinds of cry that are out there and then address the issue of the cry. I don't think we could study any other prophet (other than Jesus) in order to really see the heart of a prophet.

Let's continue with **Jeremiah 8:19: ".... because of them that dwell in a far country: *Is* not the LORD in Zion? *is* not her king in her? Why have they provoked me to anger with their graven images, *and* with strange vanities?"** Now the graven images are things that they erected as gods. God became irritated with this people because they had conjured up graven images. Where was the voice of the prophets? Where was the heart of the prophets? Where were the prophets when all of this was going on? God brought judgment on this activity, but the prophets declared this was not a time of judgment. They were saying that there is not going to be famine or anything else at that time but the prophet Jeremiah had released that word by the mind of God.

When people are engaged in this level of idolatry, the prophet is supposed to stand up. The prophet is supposed to declare truth and it is the prophet that should rise up with a rebuke in his mouth. This is important to understand. As a prophet of God, your life has to be rebuke proof in order to be able to rise up to obey the word of God and to issue out a rebuke. Otherwise you and I have no right to rebuke anyone. We are not in a position to if our lives are messed up.

God had a problem with the prophets that were not rebuking because their lives were not rebuke proof and they were actually doing things that did not reflect God. Jeremiah, on the other hand, had to make sure that he was on point. There had to be a separation between prophets and prophets. God had to separate genuine prophets from false prophets and He had to also separate genuine prophets from prophets that were in error.

Let's look at this in **Jeremiah 5:11-14: "For the house of Israel and the house of Judah have dealt very treacherously against me, saith the LORD. They have belied the LORD, and said, _It is_ not he; neither shall evil come upon us; neither shall we see sword nor famine: And the prophets shall become wind, and the word _is_ not in them: thus shall it be done unto them. Wherefore thus saith the LORD God of**

hosts, Because ye speak this word, behold, I will make my words in thy mouth fire, and this people wood, and it shall devour them."

God is talking to Jeremiah and saying to him, "Jeremiah you have to rise up and speak this word;" indicating that God probably gave the same word to other prophets that would not carry it. Remember, God does not talk to false prophets; so these that He is referring to in this passage are not false prophets, but prophets that were in error. Notice what God said to the prophets in error in **verse 13, "And the prophets shall become wind, and the word is not in them."** Now if we as prophets and prophetic people do not live our lives to God's standard, we become nothing more than a bag of wind. We are without excuse because if we do not have the heart of a prophet, we will not hear God on these kinds of issues.

Now in **verse 14, "Wherefore thus saith the LORD God of hosts, Because ye speak this word, behold, I will make my words in thy mouth fire...."** This is the separation between authentic prophets and ones that are in error. God did not say that He was going to make Jeremiah's words as fire. He said that He was making His words fire. Remember, God was talking to Jeremiah about speaking a specific word. If you and I do not have a life that matches God's standard, we are nothing more than a bag of wind (a puff). But if we do everything in our power to live up to His standard, God says He will make your words fire and the people that you are speaking to wood (....*I will make my words in thy mouth fire, and this people wood, and it shall devour them..*).

When it comes to the prophetic, God is not joking around with us. As a prophet if you are on point with God, your heart is right with God, and He has given you authority over a people – whether it is over a group of people or even one person - your words are death to them and will devour them. They won't be able to figure out why they cannot come up from where they are. It will be because your mouth is on them.

When we look at the New Testament, there is a point in the Day of Judgment where, according to the word, we will give an account of every word that comes out of our mouths. **Matthew12:36-37: "But I say unto you, That every idle word that men shall speak, they shall give account thereof in the day of judgment. For by thy words thou shalt be justified, and by thy words thou shalt be condemned."** This means that we better know what we are talking about because these are God's people and God has given us authority over His people. Therefore, you and I have to come to a point where we are saying what God is saying.

Remember, we are talking about the heart of Jeremiah, a genuine prophet. God is hurt when His people are hurt. We covered this passage in **Jeremiah. 8:20-21: "The harvest is past, the summer is ended, and we are not saved. For the hurt of the daughter of my people am I hurt; ....."** The heart of the prophet is this: *"If you are hurt – I am hurt"*. When you share your hurt with me and I am not hurt also, it is because my heart has become callous; not against you, but against God.

How can God's people hurt and we not get involved with the hurt? A tremendous question is asked of us in **Jeremiah 8:22: *"Is there* no balm in Gilead; *is there* no physician there? why then is not the health of the daughter of my people recovered?"** God is asking you and me about the condition of our area of authority. Is there no balm in your area? Fire functions two ways: it could burn to a cleansing or it could burn to destruction and that is what is in the mouth of prophets. Are we cleansing or are we killing people with our tongues?

We are real life prophets; we are just as much a prophet as Elijah was. As we wake up in the mornings we must ask ourselves, "Will life or will death come out of my mouth today?" Will we cause someone to live today? Then who do we target to speak life into today. I have to keep checking your pulse with **Jeremiah 8:18-22** because if you see me in trouble or if I see you in trouble, we have to be able to speak words of life into each other and ensure the corresponding actions of the life follow the words that we speak. There is no distance in the realm of the spirit; so you do not have to be in my presence or I in yours for words of life to be released.

Pastors, you have a major assignment in making sure those that you call to walk alongside you are examined because if they speak death to someone else, they will also speak death to you if you make them mad enough. Do you have a Gehazi or do you have an Elisha walking beside you? **2 Kings 5:25-27: "But he went in, and stood before his master. And Elisha said unto him, Whence** *comest thou,* **Gehazi? And he said, Thy servant went no whither. And he said unto him, Went not mine heart** *with thee,* **when the man turned again from his chariot to meet thee?** *Is it* **a time to receive money, and to receive garments, and oliveyards, and vineyards, and sheep, and oxen, and menservants, and maidservants? The leprosy therefore of Naaman shall cleave unto thee, and unto thy seed for ever. And he went out from his presence a leper** *as white as snow.*"

A demonstration of Elisha's heart is found in **2 Kings 2:2: "And Elijah said unto Elisha, Tarry here, I pray thee; for the LORD hath sent me to Bethel. And Elisha said** *unto him,* **As the LORD liveth, and** *as* **thy soul liveth, I will not leave thee. So they went down to Bethel."** Pastors you have to know who is walking with you. Anyone that walks close to me has to be able to speak life to people; otherwise we are working against each other. Find out the type of words your pastors or set gifts are speaking. Are they speaking prosperity (which are words of life) or do they speak words of healing? Whatever kind of word of life they speak, adopt those words. Learn to adopt the same kind of word that your man or woman of God releases into the atmosphere; otherwise you can never come along side of them. If you don't do this, you can never speak on their behalf.

Anyone that we do not see often at our church and is not present to hear the words flowing out of my mouth cannot speak here. Why? It is because we are not going to be saying the same thing. After I have been a balm in our church, they will come behind me and be a bomb. Now you have to decide if you are going to be a balm, a healing solution or a bomb, a destructive force.

This is powerful! Let us continue with **Jeremiah 1:4-5: "Then the word of the LORD came unto me, saying, Before I formed thee in the belly I knew thee; and before thou camest forth out of the womb I sanctified thee, and I ordained thee a prophet unto the nations."** Prior to coming out of the womb, you were set apart and we have to make sure that our lives compliment the purpose for which we were set apart. Jeremiah tries to give God an excuse. **Jeremiah 1:6: "Then said I, Ah, Lord GOD! behold, I cannot speak: for I *am* a child."** But we have no excuse because God can do anything except fail and lie. The reason He cannot fail and the reason that He cannot lie is because if He says it, it will come to pass. His word will never fall to the ground.

Now look at what God said to him. **Jeremiah 1:7-8: "But the LORD said unto me, Say not, I *am* a child: for thou shalt go to all that I shall send thee, and whatsoever I command thee thou shalt speak. Be not afraid of their faces: for *I am* with thee to deliver**

thee, saith the LORD." There should be no hesitation or fear. Your hesitation may be fear and fear is only a lie against the truth. God talks to Jeremiah about what He has called him to do. **Jeremiah 1:9-10: "Then the LORD put forth his hand, and touched my mouth. And the LORD said unto me, Behold, I have put my words in thy mouth. See, I have this day set thee over the nations and over the kingdoms, to root out, and to pull down, and to destroy, and to throw down, to build, and to plant."** What does "see" mean in this passage? It means **look**; I have already set you over the stuff. I have set you over nations and kingdoms already. Glory Be To His Holy Name!

The end of the passage tells us our obligations: **"to root out, and to pull down, and to destroy, and to throw down, to build, and to plant."** And when we root out, pull down, destroy or throw down, we are under obligation to build and plant. We cannot tear down without building back up.

The first thing that God is going to deal with you about is how do you see? Look at **Jeremiah 1:11-12: "Moreover the word of the LORD came unto me, saying, Jeremiah, what seest thou?"** After God let him know about everything else, God said now Jeremiah what do you see? This is the part that many of us miss. Look at Jeremiah's reply; **"And I said, I see a rod of an almond tree".** He did not say that I see a rod and that was it; he gave details about it being of an almond tree. Then God said, **"Then said the LORD unto me, Thou**

hast well seen: for I will hasten my word to perform it." God told him that He will hasten His word to perform it because he had seen well.

God tested Jeremiah's seeing in the next three chapters. God showed Jeremiah what happened in the destruction and the restoration of the earth to see if he still saw well. **Jeremiah 4:23-26: "I beheld the earth, and, lo, *it* was without form, and void; and the heavens, and they *had* no light. I beheld the mountains, and, lo, they trembled, and all the hills moved lightly. I beheld, and, lo, *there was* no man, and all the birds of the heavens were fled. I beheld, and, lo, the fruitful place was a wilderness, and all the cities thereof were broken down at the presence of the LORD, *and* by his fierce anger."**

When Jeremiah was born, the earth was already restored; now God is showing him what happened before Adam. I saw the earth and after I saw it, I saw it again and it was without form and void. I saw the heavens and then I saw it and the light was gone. I saw the mountains and then I saw them move. He was giving a description of what he saw and then what he saw was gone.

As a prophet you must see what is not there. If you cannot see what is not there, you are not going to know what God wants to make. If you see it as darkness now, God wants to make it light. If you see people messed up now, God wants to clean them up. If you heard what God said, what does God want to make?

The assignment of the prophet is to see what is! Jeremiah saw. Once he saw and God tested him in his seeing, then God understood that his heart was right and that his ears had no problems. If you cannot see, that means that your ears are not open and you are going to say the wrong stuff. God will say some things and to the natural mind, you cannot even imagine it. But you have to be able to hear what God says, put vision to what He said and only let your mouth say that until it comes into being. Whatever God says, He will make it good!

Review Questions:

1. What is the significance in having the heart of the prophet?

2. What is the difference between a "general word" and a "direct word"?

3. Describe what a prophet is required to do based on Jeremiah 1:10.

4. How does a prophet's heart become callous and how does that affect those they are assigned to?

Prophetic Intercession

Chapter 6

Prophetic Action and Declaration

P rophetic Intercession has to do with us as Prophetic people moving in the realm of Intercession from a prophetic stand point. Then we have prophetic action and declaration that releases God in a situation or area. When God wants to do something, he engages a prophet whom he has given regional or national authority over a land to prophetically speak forth.

What Does Prophetic Mean?

1) *Foretelling,* speaking about something in the future that God has decreed will come to pass.
2) *Forth telling,* speaking something forth for God, or becoming his voice in the earth. Usually that is something we call preparatory.

There are three reasons we release something in the earth:

Obedience to God brings a response from God.

God sometimes requires something from us in order to get what he said he would do. God require a prophetic act and a prophetic declaration. There are moments of obedience that God require for us to do something he has released. We don't always know why God wants us to do something he just wants it done. Naaman was told to go dip in the Jordan seven times without any further explanation; yet he was expected to obey that prophetic act.

Prophetic Acts:

a. Moses at the Red Sea was told to lift his rod that was a prophetic act.
b. Moses again was told to put his rod up and as long as the rod was up Israel was winning the battle or prevailed, but when it came down they began to lose; **Exodus 17**: that was a prophetic act. Hear the principle of how this prophetic Act works: You do something in the earth realm, God does something in the heaven realm and there is a manifestation that happens in the earth realm. This is that seed sowing principle or the principle of reciprocity. What we do is in obedience to God, and then heaven can respond, causing something in earth realm to happen. The principle is this, there is something

happening in the spirit realm that cannot be broken until earth obeys. The Rod represented the delegated authority in the earth and Moses was to life up the Rod that represented the authority of God and when that happened Israel prevailed and when it was not lifted up Israel was beginning to be defeated.

Prophetic Declarations:

There is something about decreeing things in the earth that causes heaven to establish it. **Job 22:27-28: "Thou shalt make thy prayer unto him, and he shall hear thee, and thou shalt pay thy vows. Thou shalt also decree a thing, and it shall be established unto thee: and the light shall shine upon thy ways."**

Faith releases God.

Hope and Faith Are Partners.

If your hope is bigger than your faith, then you can strain your faith trying to reach your hope that you are not developed for. Creating a hope or an image in your thinking that someday you would like to achieve will assure that you will come into it if you apply faith principles with it. You must start with where you are in reference to your faith. What I mean by that is you have to identify where or what level your faith is already working and then start at that point believing and developing.

If we will have "The God kind of faith", we will need to go back to the faith teaching of Jesus and seeing God and how he functioned in his faith operation. Since Jesus is saying to us "have faith in God" or have the God kind of faith then it is obvious that the kind of faith Jesus used was the same kind that God used. If Jesus said the "God kind of Faith", then are there other kinds? Yes!

What kinds of faith photos are there?

- **Great Faith**-Matthew 8:5-10
- **Little Faith**-Math 14:22; Luke: 12:28
- **Weak Faith** -Romans 4:19
- **Strong Faith**- Romans 4:20
- **No Faith**-Mark 4:40
- **Dead Faith**-James 2:20
- **Unfeigned Faith**- 1Timothy 1:5

We were originally created with the God-kind of faith, but lost it when Adam sinned. The good news is, Jesus redeemed us and the God kind of faith was restored in us. **Romans 12:3 "...as God hath dealt to every man the measure of faith."**

Let's look at how the God Kind of Faith works:

Mark 11:12-14 "And on the morrow, when they were come from Bethany, he was

hungry: And seeing a fig tree afar off having leaves, he came, if haply he might find anything thereon: and when he came to it, he found nothing but leaves; for the time of figs was not *yet.* And Jesus answered and said unto it, No man eat fruit of thee hereafter for ever. And his disciples heard *it.*"

- Jesus had a Need/Desire-**"he was hungry"**

- He saw the answer to his Need-**"Seeing a fig tree afar off"**

- Jesus set his expectation to Receive-**"He came if haply he might find anything there on"**

- Jesus spoke to what did not produce-**"No man eat fruit of thee here after forever"**

- He set his expectation again on what he said next and made sure he was heard

There are several components that are necessary for you to function at the level of production.

Diligence: you must be diligent in your assignment that God gives you and in what God says to you. One of the greatest pitfalls of potential faith walkers is they are tempted to side step or not continue in their faith-filled actions. There has to be a continuing of the initial steps of faith.

Eliminate Faith Enemies: You have to have a holy lifestyle and not tolerate faith's enemies. Many people walk and talk faith, but live a compromising lifestyle that causes faith not to work. Some of faith's enemies includes: works of the flesh, lust of the flesh, pride of life and lust of other things entering in choke the work and makes the word of faith unfruitful.

When God dealt with me about the miracle of the "Empty Envelope," I did not think of it as a miracle happening. I thought more of wanting to give into something that I could not give into. Knowing that some would need to copy this process, I want to give you some steps:

- Name Your Seed's Directions- (You have to want to give into something away from you in order to change your financial picture) Your faith needs a target. What is the object of your faith? **Isaiah 55: 10-11 "For as the rain cometh down, and the snow from heaven, and returneth not thither, but watereth the earth, and maketh it bring forth and bud, that it may give seed to the sower, and bread to the eater: So shall my word be that goeth forth out of my mouth: it shall not return unto me void, but it**

shall accomplish that which I please, and it shall prosper *in the thing whereto I sent it.*"
- Name your amount on the envelope before saying anything.
- Know how much you can believe for, not how much you would like to give.
- Declare aloud what you believe based on your reason for giving.
- Establish your foundation that makes this true **(2 Corithians 9:10** Now he who gives seed to the sower)
- Cast the care of this on God
- Realize that what you are believing for may come little by little or in one lump
- Don't tell God where or how to bring it in
- Release your faith based on all of the above.
- Establish Corresponding Action

Speaking God's Word releases his creativity that lives in that word spoken.

What is real Prophetic Intercession?

Prophets don't intercede as Intercessors might. Intercessors go to God on behalf of the people, but prophets go the people on behalf of God. The Prophet's orders never changes. Therefore, when the prophet is told by God to make declarations in/to the earth, the people, the region or nation, they get the benefit. Prophetic declaration or prophetic intercession is when Prophets speak into the atmosphere causing something to happen.

Example of Prophetic Intercession:

> *Ezekiel 37:1-4: "The hand of the LORD was upon me, and carried me out in the spirit of the LORD, and set me down in the midst of the valley which was full of bones, And caused me to pass by them round about: and, behold, there were very many in the open valley; and, lo, they were very dry. And he said unto me, Son of man, can these bones live? And I answered, O Lord GOD, thou knowest. Again he said unto me, Prophesy upon these bones, and say unto them, O ye dry bones, hear the word of the LORD."*

This is a clear example of Prophetic Intercession. This is something that God would do with a prophet. Look closely; **"The hand of the LORD was upon me, and** (1) **carried me out in the spirit of the LORD,** and (2) **set me down in the midst of the valley which was full of bones,** and (3) **caused me to pass by them round**

about." This is what I call the threefold preparation process of prophetic intercession.

1. **God Carried Ezekiel out** in the Spirit of the Lord where he could see from a different advantage point. Many times we try to see from where we understand in our thinking, which could be only in the first dimension, but God wants us to see from the realm of the Spirit. We have to see things from their advantage point in order for us to be effective.

2. **God set Ezekiel Down** in the midst of that situation that he was going to speak to. Unless Ezekiel, you or I come in the midst of the situation, we cannot speak to it as one that will prophetically intercede prophetically. We must be speaking from the inside to prophetically declare a thing. If we are called to youth, we have to get in the realm where they are and feel what they feel in order to pray from their advantage point.

3. **God caused Ezekiel to pass** by it round about. God wanted Ezekiel to see the situation from every side and not miss any possible angle of intercession or prophetic declarations. You and I cannot possibly speak to a nation that we have no

information on. God has always given the
Prophets information on the nation he
wanted them to speak to. **Ezekiel 37:7** said,
**"So I prophesied as I was commanded: and
as I prophesied, there was a noise, and
behold a shaking, and the bones came
together, bone to his bone."** Therefore,
Ezekiel prophetically declared to that nation
what God said or health and healing could
not come to it.

It must be understood that just anybody cannot
prophetically intercede for a city, region or nation. You
have to be called to assignment. Sometimes God calls a
church or a group of people to a particular assignment.
As a corporate body, we would have to do that
assignment together and prophetically declare to that
nation what God is saying. Remember: the prophet has
the ability to release God's creative ability in a nation or
situation where others don't have the ability to release
the same thing.

Isaiah was given an assignment to prophetically
declare in a certain nation. Isaiah said while he was in
the midst of prophesying and paused the prophecy to
declared "I will say to the north, Give up; and to the
south, Keep not back: bring my sons from far, and my
daughters from the ends of the earth; Even every one
that is called by my name: for I have created him for my
glory, I have formed him; yea, I have made him". We
have to see that God has given us intercessory power

and authority to speak to the nations or to our region. This is Prophetic Intercession. Not everyone has the authority to speak on their own behalf.

Review Questions:

1. What are the three things prophets are to release into the earth?

2. What is forth telling?

3. What is foretelling?

4. What do prophets have the ability to release?

5. What is the difference between an intercessor and a prophetic intercessor?

6. Name the different levels of faith.

7. What are two components needed to see a successful level of productivity in your faith?

Conquering Your Battle Ground

Chapter
7

Understanding the Battle Ground

There are times that we go through things in our personal life, ministry or even on our jobs and we sometimes wonder if it is us, the devil or even God taking us through something to teach us. First of all, God does not tempt or try us. The Bible says in **James 1:14 "But every man is tempted, when he is drawn away of his own lust and enticed."**

I believe we have to start to understand what is God and what is not. Through many situations, toil and snares, we suffer challenges; yet we have to identify who is behind it all so we will know who to fight. Many times we fight each other because we think it is our brother, sister, husband or maybe even our wives. We think such things even though we know **Ephesians 6:12 "For we wrestle not against flesh and blood, but against principalities, against powers, against**

the rulers of the darkness of this world, against spiritual wickedness in high *places.*"

Most of us are not aware of our battle ground or where the attack is coming from. We have not been taught to do battle and no wonder we are clueless of where it's coming from. We have been trained to receive blessing and all good things which is good. However we have to know that there is an enemy out there and, at one point or another, you will need to fight. Please be advised you will not always have to fight as in warfare, but sometimes it may the good fight. Another time it may be a serious battle where you have to take something by force; **"And from the days of John the Baptist until now the kingdom of heaven suffereth violence, and the violent take it by force." Matthew 11:12**

As a result, we have developed a welfare mentality and I believe God is preparing us to understand the battleground where we win every time. Some of us that may have had particular experiences in God know something about fighting, therefore we have developed a mentality that everybody is after us which is just as bad as having a welfare mentality always expecting someone to give us something (anything). When we look at these two mindsets we realize that everybody is not against us and God is not some cosmic Santa Clause that is going to give us everything that we want regardless of whether we worked for it or not. At one point or another we need to get our believer working and believe for things vs. having God to just hand us things all the time without us exercising our faith. Remember whatever kind of battle it may be, we will have to walk by faith.

God gave me the assignment of making sure that you and I are ready for the battle ground by way of understanding and prophetically declaring. God spoke to me about making sure that we understood the battleground. God explained there is a battle going on whether you and I understand it or not and you and I are literally the prize. God intends to win, but He needs our cooperation to do so. We have not understood the battleground; therefore, Satan was able to lure us without us consciously knowing where we were going.

Some of you are in a battle right now and some of you have already fought some battles. Some of you feel like you won, some feel like you lost and some feel like you did not win or lose; you were just engaged in a fight. Two major reasons for our defeat is that we 1) did not understand the battle ground and, 2) we have been lured onto those grounds and, consequently, ended up looking like a defeated foe. We are not defeated foes; we simply did not understand what we were fighting for, why we were fighting or why we are even engaged in this battle.

Have you ever had some kind of a relationship (i.e. brother/sister, husband/wife etc.) and you constantly have the same kind of battles with them and you question, "Why are we even having this battle?" You wonder, "Why are we engaged in this conversation; we have known each other all this time and we are still right here? What is going on with this? Why are we still at this place of conflict, still arguing about money, still arguing about bills and debt?" We have already agreed to stay on our budget and to get out of debt. "Why are we still arguing about why you keep spending and why I am so tight with the money?" The answer is because we did not understand the battleground. Any battle that you go into and you neglect to understand, it must be repeated.

God gave me instructions about the battleground. I know that you want me to tell you the battleground is your mind (and maybe I will), but I am coming from a different perspective at this moment. Let me explain something about me. When I was a child and got into a conflict, I knew that I could not fight so I would always take the first punch knowing I may not get another chance. Then I would run. At this point you'd have to catch me if you wanted to hit me back. I could not fight nor could I run well. However, it didn't matter how big you were because I was going to take the first swing. The devil does the same thing. You and I are wondering how the devil got that close to us and now we need to win the battle of our mind. He took the first swing and we left him an opening. How in the world did you and I get into so much trouble?

Seduced By Our Enemy

We were seduced by an enemy that suckered us into a battle. The only thing that we have ever heard was that the mind (internal) was the battleground. We have been taught for years that our mind was the battleground and that is all we understood. Please understand that is one of the battlegrounds. But before the enemy can get that close, you have to be seduced into coming close enough where he can even have access to your mind.

Key Point:

"Every man is tempted when he is drawn away and enticed." James 1:15

When you are drawn away (not lead) you were seduced. Check out the meaning of the word seduce: *–verb (used with object),*

- To lead astray, as from duty, rectitude, or the like; corrupt.
- To persuade or induce to have sexual intercourse.
- To lead or draw away, as from principles, faith, or allegiance: *He was seduced by the prospect of gain.*
- To win over; attract; entice: *a supermarket seducing customers with special sales.*

This should give us an understanding of what has happened to us and how we went from peace to gradual chaos. I think by now you understand why I'm approaching the battleground from these two perspectives:

1.   The battle of position (External Battle)

2.   The battle of the mind (Internal Battle)

I want to take it from a different perspective. I want to talk about the external battle-ground before I talk about the internal battleground, which is in our mind. The word of God tells us that we have peace. **John 14:27: "Peace I leave with you, my peace I give unto you: not as the world giveth, give I unto you. Let not your heart be troubled, neither let it be afraid."** Yet we know that a battle is going on and we are conscious of the battle. How can you have peace in a battle? It is possible!

I don't know about you but I have been through some battles. I don't think that you can tell me about a battle that I have not been through. I have been through some of the best battles. I can't think of any battle where the devil has not been trying to (1) count us out and (2) shut us down. The only way that he can do that is to get inside of us because the only way to shut down the plant is to get inside the plant. Please know the devil does not start inside you. He has no access to you from the inside because God has taken residence in you and me. That is the reason for his spirit of seduction. Remember, there is a progression in the battleground.

- Progression One: **Regression**
- Progression Two: **Suppression**
- Progression Three: **Depression**
- Progression Four: **Oppression**
- Progression Five: **Obsession**
- Progression Six: **Possession**

This external battle is designed by the enemy to gain access to the inside where he can control you and his ultimate goal is to gain control over your will, which is the strongest force in the earth.

The Internal Battle Ground

We need to understand these battlegrounds. There is an external battleground that the enemy has summoned us to. Now I know that this has never happened to any of you, but the only time that I felt intimidated was when I ran into somebody else's house to fight. This only happened when the person hit me first. I thought, "It's not going down like this; he used my game plan and ran." At the time I had a moment of insanity because I ran after him. When he went into his house, I pursued him. When I arrived in his house, his thought process changed and he felt that he was in safety. That was not the case because I immediately tackled him and beat him up on the floor of his house. I felt intimidated, however, because his brothers and sisters were in the house and his mother was sitting on the sofa. When I came to myself, I realized the trouble that I was in because none of my folks were around. When I elected to run into what I did not know would become a battleground, I did feel intimidated but intimidation did not hit beforehand.

That is what the devil does. He lures us into his battleground and defeats us every time. He is supposed to because it is his battleground and God never told us to go there. That battleground was selected by the devil and we ran after it or into it and many times to our demise.

Remember, God has planned no defeat for you and me. We are "more than Conquerors through Christ Jesus." Then why do we feel defeated? We closed the door on what happened to us and we made that the end. When that person hit me and I took the hit, what if I had called that the end? A moment of insanity refused to let me call that the end. What is it that you are calling the end when God never intended for that to be the end. You accepted that as defeat when God never considered that the end. What if God would have called Adam's defeat the end? Then there would have never been grace for you and me.

My assignment is to prepare you for a battleground. If given access to your battleground, the enemy tries to stagnate, paralyze and to shut you down. Your battleground is your battleground. We think that the enemy can just show up when he wants to but, we have to give him access. Our battleground is not somewhere the enemy can just show up, we give him access when we leave a door open for him to choose the battleground. If you recall when there was going to be a (physical) fight, you and I would choose where the battleground was going to be. Remember what we use to do as children? We would say to our opponent, "Meet me behind the school at 3 o'clock." At that point we have chosen the battle- ground. It is always a mistake for you to choose the battleground and I show up, but that is what we do. The Devil selects the battleground and when you and I show up, that is an automatic defeat. With all the power of God that is on us, when we let the Devil select the battleground, it is an automatic defeat.

God has planned no defeat for us. This might be a tremendous revelation for us because we are trying to figure out why is it that we have obeyed God and been defeated. Any defeat that is planned for you is a judgment against you. God did not plan your defeat. Now we want to question what happened. How did we obey God and still become defeated? One of the things that you should know and remember is that faith without obedience does not manifest victory in your life. That means that if you and I call ourselves having faith regarding something and we are not in step with obedience then that does not manifest any victory.

Literally what has happened is that the Devil has called you on a battleground and you were the victim. Why? Because you did not hear God say come to this ground. You were not led by the Spirit of God to come to this ground. You were following the enemy on the ground and there was no victory for you.

The best place in the Bible that we can go to see this is Jesus in the wilderness in Matthew chapter 4. He was led up into the wilderness by the Spirit. This is a capital S indicating that He was led up into the wilderness by the Holy Spirit to be tempted of the Devil. **Matthew 4:1: "Then was Jesus led up of the Spirit into the wilderness to be tempted of the devil."** God selected Jesus' battleground and the devil showed up

The tempter is not always present. We see that in **Matthew 4:3 "And when the tempter came to him, he said, If thou be the Son of God, command that these stones be made bread."** We often think that we have experienced complete victory, but what has happened is that the tempter has not come yet. Now when the tempter came to Jesus, the tempter "said" – the temper uses words; he is trying to reach your mind. The tempter does not have any access at this point because Jesus has not given him any. At this point he only has an **external** battleground. The ground that the tempter really wants to conquer is your **internal** battleground. Your battle is not an external battleground and you cannot give him access to your battleground, because it is an **internal** battleground.

However, we are always giving him access to our battleground; he cannot get access unless we give it to him. Remember, there is an **external** battleground and there is an **internal** battleground and with this external battle ground you can win every time.

If God ever tells you or leads you into a battle, you have already won. The devil is the defeated one. Assess the battle that you are going through now. If you are having a battle in your mind, you have already let the devil go too far. He is <u>not</u> supposed to get that far. You have already been lured to the battleground that the tempter has selected. If you are in the battleground that God has selected, the tempter has to come because he is not there when you get there.

Remember, when I talked about meeting another child behind the school at 3. I chose the battleground. God is trying to educate us in the battleground to keep you in charge of the battle. He wants to win, however, He is not going to win if you cave in and quit. God wants us to win every time. God wants us to keep a peace of mind in the battle. When God chooses the battleground, you may not see how it is going to work but you just stand on the fact that God <u>said</u> and keep standing on that.

My daughter had a situation that caused me to start to imagine what she was going through. One of the items was a hospital bill of over $600,000.00. She went on and on talking about the bill and other associated matters. At first I tried to imagine what she was saying, but I had to shut that down because I cannot afford to imagine anything that is raising itself above the knowledge of God. When you are on the battleground, don't imagine, especially if you are trying to help someone else fight. She did not choose for those things to happen to her and I did not have any answers at first. However, so much good came out of that bad situation, it could not possibly solely been the devil. This is what I finally said, "You will not have to pay that bill." I did not have any basis to say that except the Spirit of God revealed it to me. I am seeing the devil being defeated over and over again in her situation and I decided that I will not be moved by circumstances because God <u>said</u>. Now since God gave me that word I am going to remain sensitive to the rest of what God is saying so we know what to do. The bottom line is she did not have to pay it. The government did not have to pay. The ones that were responsible for it paid. She took advantage of everything that they offered because this was God defending her.

When the devil calls you on a ground and you don't show up, God will show up and God will make them pay double. When you are in that kind of position, you have to be quiet. IF you are not conscious of the battleground and you don't know what to say, DON'T SAY ANYTHING. Just say to God, "I know you see this.", and trust God and you can win every battle.

You winning every battle is not unattainable. Jesus won every battle but the one He surrendered. Jesus said, "No one takes my life, I give it up." He said this in **John 10:18 "No man taketh it from me, but I lay it down of myself. I have power to lay it down, and I have power to take it again. This commandment have I received of my Father."** Remember, when they came to arrest Him and he asked them, "Whom seek ye?" They said, "Jesus of Nazareth." Jesus had eleven of His disciples with him and only Judas was missing. When he answered them saying, "I am He", they all fell to the ground. We find the account of this in **John 18:4-6, 4 "Jesus therefore, knowing all things that should come upon him, went forth, and said unto them, Whom seek ye? They answered him, Jesus of Nazareth. Jesus saith unto them, I am *he*. And Judas also, which betrayed him, stood with them. As soon then as he had said unto them, I am *he*, they went backward, and fell to the ground."** He did not put His hands on anyone. He just said, "I am He" and they fell out under the power of God.

He then waits for them to come back to themselves and said in **John 18:8 8 "Jesus answered, I have told you that I am *he*: if therefore ye seek me, let these go their way:"** Jesus asked them to let the eleven go and to take Him and they did, but the truth of the matter is that they did not take Him. He went with them willingly. He could have said the same thing and released the same power and got away, but He understood that it was time now. What time was He talking about? He understood that it was time for Him to go to the devils battleground. He went to the place where it was already clear that He would be slaughtered there. He allowed them to take Him. He allowed them to beat Him. He allowed them to do it all because at any given moment He could have asked for more than twelve legions of angels to come and get him and they would have showed up so the battle was always His, even at that place of Calvary. He could have won the battle even then but He **voluntarily** became the sacrifice.

I do not want to hurt your feeling or damage your religion, but I want you to understand that you choose the battleground. You and I wear a cross, but we don't know the meaning of it. It is not a holy symbol, but it is a symbol that represents the place where He gave His life. It's a symbol that represents what happened, but you and I embrace it as a holy symbol. The Star of David was a holy symbol--the cross is not, no more than the serpent in the wilderness was a holy symbol; it merely represented Christ. This is something that we must understand or we will be defeated in our battleground. A bad perception of a great reality is not any good. When we go into a battle and have a bad perception of a great reality, it is not any good. We don't know why we are there and as a result we do not understand our battleground. We, therefore, minimize that whole experience. When we have a moment in the battleground, we have to understand that we have come to win and we must come to rely on the grace of God. We don't come to rely on the grace of God as if we can go ahead and lay down in sin because God will forgive me – not in the battleground. If we do, we are about to be defeated in the battleground. We do rely on the grace of God to empower us to defeat the devil at this point. We show up on the battleground as a victor in the battleground.

The battleground has been selected by God. You stepped into that battleground because that is the ground where God wanted His grace to show up so that you could defeat your enemy there. Here is the problem; we rely on the wrong grace in the right place. There is a grace that empowers. This is the grace for grown up folks in God because they know how to sling their Word, handle their shield and where to put their helmet. Does this mean that you throw away the grace that pardons us of the sin that we committed? No, we don't throw that away. It has its proper place but that place is not on the battle ground.

2 Corinthian 10:3-5: "For though we walk in the flesh, we do not war after the flesh: (For the weapons of our warfare *are* not carnal, but mighty through God to the pulling down of strong holds;) Casting down imaginations, and every high thing that exalteth itself against the knowledge of God, and bringing into captivity every thought to the obedience of Christ;" We see in verse 5 the casting down of imaginations, remember the imagination is in the mind and that is your internal battle ground. So when the enemy speaks words to you, he speaks to gain access to your battleground, which is your thought realm. Some of us have already been seduced on this particular battleground. We followed the bait to come to this battleground.

Check this out in **Philippians 2:5-10 "Let this mind be in you, which was also in Christ Jesus: Who, being in the form of God, thought it not robbery to be equal with God: But made himself of no reputation, and took upon him the form of a servant, and was made in the likeness of men: And being found in fashion as a man, he humbled himself, and became obedient unto death, even the death of the cross. Wherefore God also hath highly exalted him, and given him a name which is above every name: That at the name of Jesus every knee should bow, *of things* in heaven, and *things* in earth, and *things* under the earth;"** We need the mind of Christ Jesus, but some of us have already been drawn away by our on lust so that we can be slaughtered in this particular battleground.

One of the things that we have to do is to overcome this is to get delivered from people. God spoke to me regarding this in my private prayer time and I found myself repenting. I came to the understanding that I have nothing to prove to any man. Many of us battle with this because we feel that we have to prove this or that to somebody and that is the seduction. We want to become a star because we have something to prove. We want mega money because we have something to prove. We are putting on a show for husbands, wives, Bishops, Pastors and people in our circle of influence because we have something to prove. We want to be on television because we have something to prove. We want to own things because we have something to prove. But we have nothing to prove and I hit that reality in my prayer time. I have nothing to prove to anyone. My soul purpose for being in the earth is to bring glory to God, my Father in heaven.

You and I have danced the dance and sang the song trying to prove something to somebody. We have one thing to prove and that is to God alone. We have to realize that God alone is great. Our assignment is to tear the works of the devil down and in doing so our Father will be glorified. God does not like attention getters. We have one purpose and one purpose alone. At my church we are about to change some things. We are no longer having any services to prove something to somebody. God can move whenever He wants for as long as He wants and if it is too long for anybody, they can leave and come back next week. This does not mean that we will hold up the program with flesh. It means as long as God is moving, we will step out of the way and let Him move and we have to know the difference. When you and I are putting on a show for somebody, God does not like it because He will not share His glory with anybody. We have to make sure that everything that we do and every breath that we breathe glorifies God. Too many of us have already fallen for the bait and we must settle this today.

Do you realize how many men and even Holy Ghost pimps, try to see how many women they can get just because they feel that they have something to prove to somebody? God says I am not glorified in that because our sole purpose is to bring Him Glory. Remember **Phillipians 2:5-7 "Let this mind be in you, which was also in Christ Jesus: Who, being in the form of God, thought it not robbery to be equal with God: But made himself of no reputation, and took upon him the form of a servant, and was made in the likeness of men:"** Verse 7, he made himself of no reputation, but we have major battles trying to prove to someone in the earth that we are great. But how does God see us? Jesus stepped down out of a holy heaven and took upon Him the form of a servant and made of himself no reputation but He became the greatest reputation in the earth. He would heal the sick and say don't tell anybody. But we heal the sick and say look what I did. But we did not do it; it was Jesus working with us confirming the word with signs and wonders. You and I did nothing but obeyed the leading of the Lord.

We live in a different reality and the only real stars are the ones that God makes, not the one we make ourselves. We have to desire to glorify God. My former pastor, Apostle Betty Peebles, who recently went home to be with the Lord coined the phrase, "Performing for an Audience of One." I was not around when she coined this phrase, but I saw it and it blessed me. Think about that, how many people are you performing for? It has been written concerning her that she has done what no other woman on the planet has done performing for an audience of one. If we look at the life of Jesus we will see that He lived what she put into words. Jesus was performing for an audience of one, His Father God. Jesus would say all of the time, "I came to do the will of my Father or I say only what I hear Him say." He was performing for an audience of one. Jesus says in **John 6:38 "For I came down from heaven, not to do mine own will, but the will of him that sent me."** He was performing for an audience of one.

Three things about the battleground that you should know and remember:

1. The battleground should always be the place that God chose

2. You should be led by the Holy Spirit into that place

3. The tempter had to come to the place that God has chosen

If you understand that you will have victory. God will lead you into your wealthy place.

I have chosen another place in the bible for you to see that God chooses the battleground. This is found in Numbers chapter 16. The scenario is that Korah has come against Moses and had chosen some choice leaders to join him in doing so. Moses is in a battle now because he realizes that people that he thought were with him were not with him. Their thought was that Moses took too much upon himself. They wanted to know, "Why do you see yourself bigger than us?" God talks to us too!

Numbers 16:15-36: "And Moses was very wroth, and said unto the LORD, Respect not thou their offering:" Moses was trying to get them into their wealthy place but now Moses is saying not to respect their offering, this is one of the reasons that I do not put my mouth on men or women of God because they can say this any time "don't respect his offering" notice that Moses says to God that he is not guilty of anything. **"I have not taken one ass from them, neither have I hurt one of them. And Moses said unto Korah, Be thou and all thy company before the LORD, thou, and they, and Aaron, tomorrow:"** This is the place where Moses selected the battle ground. Korah is wrong and he is letting Moses select a battle ground in the presence of God. This is an absolute defeat in this situation. Moses named the place and the time.

You must do the same; name the place and the time. **"And take every man his censer, and put incense in them, and bring ye before the LORD every man his censer, two hundred and fifty censers; thou also, and Aaron, each *of you* his censer. And they took every man his censer, and put fire in them, and laid incense thereon, and stood in the door of the tabernacle of the congregation with Moses and Aaron. And Korah gathered all the congregation against them unto the door of the tabernacle of the congregation:"** the door of the tabernacle was the place of the battle ground, now Moses has said where to come, 'when to come and what time to come. Korah was expecting to win but he was wrong he was going to be defeated **"and the glory of the LORD appeared unto all the congregation"**. God's glory appeared, there is a back side of the hand of God and a front side of the hand of God and you have to decide which side you want. The front side holds blessing. Which side do you want? You choose the side you want by your actions. Some of us are getting the back side of the hand of God because of our actions. We chose to fight on a battleground that God never told us to go to. You are having this battle and you lost. Most of the time we have determined that the battle was over, but it was not. Most of the time I have marked the battle as being over, but it was not because God had not determined that it was over. Remember God sets the battle. But take a look at Korah's defeat in the rest of this passage.

> **"And the LORD spake unto Moses and unto Aaron, saying. Separate yourselves from among this congregation, that I may consume them in a moment. And they fell upon their faces, and said, O God, the God of the spirits of all flesh, shall one man sin, and wilt thou be wroth with all the congregation? And the LORD spake unto Moses, saying, Speak unto the**

congregation, saying, Get you up from about the tabernacle of Korah, Dathan, and Abiram. And Moses rose up and went unto Dathan and Abiram; and the elders of Israel followed him. And he spake unto the congregation, saying, Depart, I pray you, from the tents of these wicked men, and touch nothing of theirs, lest ye be consumed in all their sins. So they got up from the tabernacle of Korah, Dathan, and Abiram, on every side: and Dathan and Abiram came out, and stood in the door of their tents, and their wives, and their sons, and their little children. And Moses said, Hereby ye shall know that the LORD hath sent me to do all these works; for *I have not done them* of mine own mind. If these men die the common death of all men, or if they be visited after the visitation of all men; *then* the LORD hath not sent me. But if the LORD make a new thing, and the earth open her mouth, and swallow them up, with all that *appertain* unto them, and they go down quick into the pit; then ye shall understand that these men have provoked the LORD. And it came to pass, as he had made an end of speaking all these words, that the ground clave asunder that *was* under them: And the earth opened her mouth, and swallowed them up, and their houses, and all the men that *appertained* unto Korah, and all *their* goods. They, and all that *appertained* to them, went down alive into the pit, and the earth closed upon them: and they perished from among the congregation. And all Israel that *were* round about them fled at the cry of them: for they said, Lest the earth swallow us up *also*. And there came out a fire from the LORD, and consumed the two hundred and fifty men that offered incense". Numbers 16:20-35

You and I have to have the right mindset; God has already set us up as winners. Many of us are going into battle but we don't have the right mindset. Have you ever watched karate or boxing movies? You may have been focused on the fight; the fight is the battle, but the best part is the mentoring. One pattern that they have in common is to never lose your temper or you will lose the fight. When you become angry, you do things to hurt yourself.

One of the things that people do when they get angry is to go out and spend money that they should not spend and they think that the devil is really going to be mad. The truth is that you only hurt yourself. Now you can't pay your mortgage or your rent or you can't pay utility bills, etc. Who did you hurt? Certainly not the devil. I have looked at many professional fights and the moment that an opponent lost their temper is the moment they begin to lose the fight. Your temper is attached to your emotions. Never allow anyone to make you angry because when that happens you have loss control of the battle.

Let's go to another place where we can see what I am talking about; **2 Corinthians 10:3-5: "For though we walk in the flesh, we do not war after the flesh:"** Why do we try to win with natural things? This is a spiritual battle and if you are in the battle, God should have called it. **"(For the weapons of our warfare *are* not carnal, but mighty through God to the pulling down of strongholds;)"** We can see from this verse that God calls the battle. You have to walk away from some things even if you think that they may call you a punk. You may think that you won the victory because you get a natural victory but you are not in a natural battle you are in a spiritual battle, so who really won? What is a strong hold? It is the place where the devil lures you into a battle at the place he chose. **"Casting down imaginations,"**- the imagination is in the mind and that is an internal battleground. Verse 5 says cast that down **"and every high thing that exalteth itself against the knowledge of God, and bringing into captivity every thought to the obedience of Christ;"** remember you have go to the battle ground that God chooses, which is external and not the one the devil wants to lure you to; which is internal. Remember my story about how I fought as a child. I would choose the battle with words. We called those words selling wolf tickets, which means I could not back up my words. I did not know that this was the way God did it. I won the battle with words most of the time and they did not know that I could not fight. David understood this principle; he used words to select the battle ground that God had chosen when he was going to fight Goliath, we see that in **1 Sam 17:37 "David said moreover, The LORD that delivered me out of the paw of the lion, and out of the paw of the bear, he will deliver me out of the hand of this Philistine. And Saul said unto David, Go, and the LORD be with thee."** You can do the same thing. You can say, "God is going to deliver me from this just like He did from the last thing that I battled with. God wants me to win against tumors, cancer, financial distress, legal matters and any other thing that exalts itself against the knowledge of God and bring that into the obedience of Christ. These things that I am facing now will be as one of those things that God has already delivered me from. God wants me to win."

David comes out with no armor on ready for battle. One of the first things that he said was "who is this uncircumcised Philistine that he should defy the armies of the living God' **1 Sam 17:26 "And David spake to the men that stood by him, saying, What shall be done to the man that killeth this Philistine, and**

taketh away the reproach from Israel? for who *is* this uncircumcised Philistine, that he should defy the armies of the living God?" David said that this uncircumcised Philistine will be like the bear and the lion. Are we not the army of the living God? We have to have the correct mindset and understand covenant. We have a covenant with the most high God.

My wife and I were praying and I became overwhelmed by the presence of God. I began to say, "To you be the glory, God." In this battleground you and I have to understand that it is Him. I became overwhelmed in His presence and I understood what He was impressing upon me from **Philippians 2:5-7 "Let this mind be in you, which was also in Christ Jesus: Who, being in the form of God, thought it not robbery to be equal with God: But made himself of no reputation, and took upon him the form of a servant, and was made in the likeness of men:"** Jesus made Himself of no reputation. I understood that you and I have nothing to prove to anybody. We have spent so much time trying to prove something to this person or that person, but we do not need to prove anything to anyone. People become ashamed because they are trying to prove things to people and when we do that, we end up disapproving God. God wants us to be ourselves, not try to prove anything to anybody. We should not try to prove anything to anybody whether we pray, preach, sing etc. When we don't have anything to prove to anybody, then God gets the glory. To God be the glory for whatever we do. If we make a mistake or say something wrong, we may become bashful and ashamed and that is because we want to prove something. If you are a singer or musician and miss a note, so what; just keep on going. Most of us won't know anyway if you don't have anything to prove to anyone.

I put pressure on me to take care of some things that I want to change in my life, and I struggled when I was trying to prove it to someone. When I decided to do it for me, I was able to make the change that I wanted. It never happened when I was doing it to prove something to other people. If you have ever done this then let me set you free. As far as I am concerned, you don't have to do one single thing to win my approval. You have my approval. You do not do things to get approval. Be who you are! The best person you can ever be is who you are. There is absolutely nothing wrong with you. You are a unique person and God wants to use your uniqueness just the way you are.

Preparation for Your Battleground

I believe that we can live a life of victory, remember it is possible for you to obey God and lose battles. I want to focus on four (4) principles that prepare you to win battles. Anything that the enemy brings against us, we can actually win every time. I believe that one of the most exciting things that we can do is to actually win the attacks that the devil brings against us. You may be one of those that desired to do some things and you know that you did not win because of the devil. This information is going to help you tremendously. The four principles will help tremendously, as we embrace them, causing us to win the battle every time is a lifestyle of prayer. God keeps pushing us until we have a lifestyle of prayer. Not just the hour a day or every other day, but a lifestyle of talking to God. God has more to say that we could imagine. Some people don't think that God has that much to say and those may be the ones that talk a lot. They talk to hear themselves talk or to impress themselves. God only talks so that He can get information to us so.

As we look at understanding the battleground, the first thing that we have to do is to recognize what Jesus did. In Matthew chapter 4 we see that Jesus was designed to come into a level of temptation. This is a battleground that God chose and it was a battle that Jesus was going to win. Sometimes we stumble onto a battleground and we are not armed or prepared to fight. Every one of us in the body of Christ is going to have a battle and if we have already been through a battle, the next one is intensified. We should not be surprised at what is going on. Jesus was led into the wilderness but He did not plan to stay there. He planned to beat the devil and come back out of the wilderness and that is what we should be doing; going into the wilderness, planning to be victorious over the devil and coming back out. Some of us go into the wilderness as if we plan to stay there.

The four principles that Jesus employed to position Himself to win ever battle are as follows:

1. He submitted himself to spiritual authority.

2. He committed to fulfill all righteousness.

3. He walked under an open heaven.

4. He received the Spirit of God and walked in the light.

These four principles are a series of things that happened before He was led by the Spirit of God into the wilderness to be tempted as described in Matthew chapter 4. All of these principles are seen in **Matthew 3:13-17 "Then cometh Jesus from Galilee to Jordan unto John, to be baptized of him. But John forbad him, saying, I have need to be baptized of thee, and comest thou to me? And Jesus answering said unto him, Suffer *it to be so* now: for thus it becometh us to fulfill all righteousness. Then he suffered him. And Jesus, when he was baptized, went up straightway out of the water: and, lo, the heavens were opened unto him, and he saw the Spirit of God descending like a dove, and lighting upon him: And lo a voice from heaven, saying, This is my beloved Son, in whom I am well pleased.?"**

Here we are, the people of God, and we are not seeing the level of victory that God wants to see in our lives. How can that be possible? It is possible. In life there are going to be some battles, but when they come up, we have to win. Winning is a decision; you don't win by chance. You have purpose in your heart that you are going to win this one and you have to do what you are supposed to be doing in order to win. Jesus is our chief example setter and He won in every area of His life. He was tempted in all points just like you and I, but He won at His battles. He did not quit when it was time to produce. We can't cave in, faint and quit. This is happening to people every day, but it is not supposed to happen to us. We are not supposed to lose—that is to say, the body of Christ. If we obey what Jesus said and did, we will have victory every time. Every time a battle came up, Jesus was already set in position to win. That is the challenge with you and I; we are not already set in position to win. Now when the battle comes up, we don't win because we were not in position to win. When I really understood this, it was only at that point that I started to win.

Let us look at what Jesus did in **Matthew 4:1-4 "Then was Jesus led up of the Spirit into the wilderness to be tempted of the devil. And when he had fasted forty days and forty nights, he was afterward an hungered. And when the tempter came to him, he said, If thou be the Son of God, command that these stones be made bread. But he answered and said, It is written, Man shall not live by bread alone, but by every word that proceedeth out of the mouth of God."** If we are going to win, we have to live by every word that proceedeth out of the mouth of God and that is going to take commitment. How do you position yourself? If we are going to live by every word that proceedeth out the mouth of God, we have to understand that is not a set place. Living by every word that proceedeth out of the mouth of God is something that is going to have to happen every day, but that is not what sets you. That is your action according to the position that you are set in. Let me give you an example of being in the right position.

Isn't it amazing that many of us want to be blessed financially but we don't do the things that positions us to be blessed financially. What position do you have to be in to be blessed financially? You must be employed; if you are not, you are not in position to be blessed financially. Another example: Maybe you want to save some money for something, but do you have a bank account? If not, you are not in position to save money. You can't have a mindset to wait until you get employed to get a bank account because that is what puts you in position to save. Get $5 and open an account; use the money you were going to spend on fast food and when you do that three times you now have $15 and you are not even working. Another example: You want to have a good marriage, but you are always spending time with the boys or the girls and they are single. You are not in position to have a good marriage, because a single person cannot tell you how to stay married.

According to **Matthew 4:1,** Jesus is led up of the Spirit into the wilderness. The first word of this verse is then. When the word "then" is used, it means that something came before or something happened before Jesus was led up. Now what we have to do is go back and find out what the "then" is there for. We know chapter four (4) is about the battle. Jesus was in the wilderness fasting and praying and He did not necessarily think about being tested of the devil. I don't think that any of us have that in mind when we are approaching our testing and certainly not our time of being tempted of the devil. I know that I did not have that in mind as I was going through my test. When you went into that test, you did not know what it was for. One of the things that amazes me is that people decide to get married, but are not prepared for the test. They only address the sweet part; you are the apple of my eye, etc. and then later they wonder "is this what I signed up for?" The second you get married, you are in position for there to be a battle even if you are not in position for the battle. If you are positioned properly, you can keep the happiness even in the mist of the battle. Remember in **Matthew. 4:1,** Jesus was happy to go into the wilderness. When you are making all of the preparation the tempter is not present. Then when you are ready, the tempter shows up and many of us are surprised. Many of us want ministry, but we do not want the process. Many of us are in business, but we don't want the process. Without the process, we are not positioned. I remember one time there was a man that wanted to go into the restaurant business and someone suggested that he go and work for one and when he did that, he did not want to own a restaurant. He just wanted to cook for one because he did not want the process. He did not want the planning, the scheduling, the marketing, the supply issues and the customers that want a free meal.

Anything that you are not positioned for will shut you down mentally and that will cause you to lose the battle. Remember, we are talking about the external battle and the internal battle. The devil attacks us on the internal battleground and that is the battleground that he has prepared. If we are positioned according to the external battleground that God has prepared, he will never be able to get to our internal battleground (our mind). He cannot get to the internal battleground until he shuts you down on the external and if you are not positioned for the battle, that's exactly what will happen. The number one mistake that we make is losing the external battle and allowing the devil access to our mind. **2 Kings 6:15-17: "And when the servant of the man of God was risen early, and gone forth, behold, an host compassed the city both with horses and chariots."** Elisha was positioned for the battle, but his servant was not so he said, **"And his servant said unto him, Alas, my master! how shall we do?"** The Prophets respond, **"And he answered, Fear not: for they that be with us *are* more than they that be with them. And Elisha prayed, and said, LORD, I pray thee, open his eyes, that he may see. And the LORD opened the eyes of the young man; and he saw: and, behold, the mountain was full of horses and chariots of fire**

round about Elisha." The servant was affected by his mental and spiritual shutdown-- he was not positioned. The Prophet asked God to open his eyes and let him see. What happened at this moment was that the Prophet that was the spiritual authority over his life spoke and he was able to see. No matter what you are going through, there is more with you than with them. God has already arranged victory for you, so it doesn't matter what the enemy has planned. All you have to do is position yourself for the battle.

This concept can also be seen when Jehoshaphat was in battle, the battle was already set against him and he did not know what to do so he had to ask God. Have you ever been already in the battle and did not know what to do; well I have. I could not run nor could I go forward and all I could do was to pray. Jehoshaphat knew that he could not run, and that's what we have to do also; don't run but do what Jehoshaphat did in **2 Chronicles 20:13-15: "And all Judah stood before the LORD, with their little ones, their wives, and their children. Then upon Jahaziel the son of Zechariah, the son of Benaiah, the son of Jeiel, the son of Mattaniah, a Levite of the sons of Asaph, came the Spirit of the LORD in the midst of the congregation; And he said, Hearken ye, all Judah, and ye inhabitants of Jerusalem, and thou king Jehoshaphat, Thus saith the LORD unto you, Be not afraid nor dismayed by reason of this great multitude; for the battle *is* not yours, but God's"** The word from God did not even come to Jehoshaphat, but to one in the congregation saying that you shall not have to fight in this battle. God has established that this is a battle and now he begins to position Jehoshaphat for it, but he has to listen to what God is saying through Jahaziel in **2 Chronicles 20:16-18: "To morrow go ye down against them: behold, they come up by the cliff of Ziz; and ye shall find them at the end of the brook, before the wilderness of Jeruel.** Ye shall not *need* to fight in this *battle*: set yourselves, stand ye *still*, and see the salvation of the LORD with you, O Judah and Jerusalem: fear not, nor be dismayed; tomorrow go out against them: for the LORD *will* be with you. And Jehoshaphat bowed his head with *his* face to the ground: and all Judah and the inhabitants of Jerusalem fell before the LORD, worshipping the LORD."** God told them to "set yourselves", "stand ye still" and "see the salvation of the LORD." What happens when the devil attacks you in the pre -attack arena He does this so that he can gain access to your thought world to shut you down spiritually, shut you down mentally and cause you to be an emotional wreck. Now you can't think or hear God, so what do you do? There is nothing that you can do except be beaten by the devil.

Can you bounce back? Yes you can. Look what Jesus did in **Matthew 3:13-17: "Then cometh Jesus from Galilee to Jordan unto John, to be baptized of him. But John forbad him, saying, I have need to be baptized of thee, and comest thou to me? And Jesus answering said unto him, Suffer *it* to be so *now*: for thus it becometh us to fulfill all righteousness. Then**

he suffered him. And Jesus, when he was baptized , went up straightway out of the water: and, lo, the heavens were opened unto him, and he saw the Spirit of God descending like a dove, and lighting upon him: And lo a voice from heaven, saying, This is my beloved Son, in whom I am well pleased." *Jesus* did four things that positioned Him for the battle. Remember, I mentioned this earlier; you are vulnerable to anyone that baptizes you. It only takes a few minutes for a person to drown. Baptizing is a risky business for pastors. I remember one occasion when I was helping a pastor baptize a 600 pound person. The baptismal pool was very small and it was old. The water was very cold because the pool was not heated and we were all cramped in that small pool. The pastor and I were totally responsible to get him under the water and back up again. The gentleman totally trusted us to take care of him. I remember thinking about that 600 pounds and realizing that we must get him down and up again because if we drop him he could drown. This gentleman was at our mercy just like Jesus was at the mercy of John.

Jesus put Himself at the mercy of John, His spiritual authority in the earth. John was the forerunner of Jesus and this is another way of saying that Jesus is the Successor of John. If I am training someone because they are to take my place, then I am their forerunner. We can look at this and actually see that when John was getting ready to be beheaded, he wanted to know that Jesus was in place. We see that in **Matthew 11:2-3:**

"Now when John had heard in the prison the works of Christ, he sent two of his disciples, And said unto him, Art thou he that should come, or do we look for another"? John sent his disciples to Jesus because he needed to know if Jesus was the one. John knew that he was about to be beheaded and he wanted to make sure because he knew that the ones that were planning to behead him did not give him life and they cannot take it away. If Jesus is the one that is to take his place and Jesus is in place, John knew that everything that was happening was OK. Remember that John's disciples followed Jesus after John left.

You cannot start ministry until you get to this point of submitting to spiritual authority. Now let's revisit what Jesus did to position Himself to win the battle. The tragedy is that the ones that are in line to be announced as John did Jesus, do not demonstrate any movement that resembles being ready to take the place of the spiritual authority. Some of the leaders in our church are called to the same battles that I am called to and more than likely by the time they get to a battleground, I have already left. But some of them end up at the battleground and have not even been to my training yet that. That means that they are not prepared for the battleground. We have to be positioned properly in order to win the battle. Remember we talked earlier about the four principles that will ensure that you win the battle every time as you implement them in your life.

They are as follows:

1. **He submitted himself to spiritual authority.**
John was the one that was to introduce Jesus.
John was here before Jesus and John was the
spiritual authority that Jesus had to check in with
and submit to because it was John's assignment
to introduce Jesus. John had Jesus' file and he had
authority to baptize him. The very first thing
that Jesus did was to submit himself under was
the hand of John and it was only after this event
that Jesus actually started his ministry. Who has
been given your file? Who has the authority to
release you into ministry? Somebody knows
exactly what your next move ought to be.
Remember, the sons of Issachar mentioned in **1
Chronicles 12:32 "And of the children of
Issachar, *which were men* that had
understanding of the times, to know what
Israel ought to do;...."** When the king has a
problem and needed information, they always
went to the Prophet to hear a prophetic word or
they went to fortune tellers to consult with
demons.

2. **Commit to fulfill all righteousness.** When Jesus
went to John to be baptized, John recognized a
baptism that Jesus was designed to bring forth in
Matthew 3:11 "I indeed baptize you with

water unto repentance: but he that cometh
after me is mightier than I, whose shoes I am
not worthy to bear: he shall baptize you with
the Holy Ghost, and *with* fire:" John wanted
that baptism of fire that Jesus was going to
introduce and John said, "I need to be baptized of
you." Jesus answered and said **"Suffer *it to be so*
now: for thus it becometh us to fulfill all
righteousness. Then he suffered him."** Jesus
was bringing in the baptism of fire and the
baptism of fire does not come first. So they both
agreed to commit to fulfill all righteousness. That
should be true for you and me. Anything that
God is for, it is our position to fulfill it. Many of
us in the body of Christ want to fulfill our
personal pleasures or all of the things that my
favorite person loves even if it causes you to
compromise the standard of God. When we do
this, we are not positioned to win. You can't
fulfill all righteousness by yourself.

Notice what Jesus said to John in verse 15 **"for
thus it becometh us to fulfill all
righteousness."** It took both of them to do it.
The spiritual authority that God has placed over
your life is designed to be a part of this with you.
Who is with you? I would be a fool to think that I
can accomplish the tremendous assignment of
this ministry by myself. I need the help of the
spiritual authority that is over me. I would also
be a fool to think that everybody has to be just

like me. Jesus said I have other sheep in **John 10:16: "And other sheep I have, which are not of this fold: them also I must bring, and they shall hear my voice; and there shall be one fold,** *and* **one shepherd."** This is confirmed in Luke when Jesus was talking to John about a person that was not with them. **Luke 9:49-50: "And John answered and said, Master, we saw one casting out devils in thy name; and we forbad him, because he followeth not with us And Jesus said unto him, Forbid** *him* **not: for he that is not against us is for us."** Jesus told John to leave him alone. Jesus is not a groupie! Everybody will not be in your group. We have to let the people of God be the people of God and leave them alone. We have to be positioned to win. In addition, I need people who have the supply for the areas that I am weak in so that we all (the entire Church) can finish strong. We all have to make it across the finish line. If I make it across the finish line by myself, I did not win. I lost because we all have to make it.

I have to be able to stand up and say we won.

Are we really committed to fulfill all righteousness? If not, Satan knows that and when you we in the heat of the battle, he calls you on it. I remember listening to great men and women of God say when they were casting out demons that Satan would rise up and say, "I have a right to be here because they asked me to be here". When they would tell the demon to come out, it would say no and the only way they could get that demon out is to get that person to repent and say that they don't want it anymore. The Holy Spirit is the same way. We have to ask Him to come in. He does not force His way in. Satan is devious when he gets us to participate in activities that invite him in. An example of those kinds of activities are office Christmas parties, happy hour etc. We may have to attend, but we do not have to participate in what the king is eating.

3. **Walk under an open heaven**. Do you realize that you could be sitting next to someone in church that is living under an open heaven and you are not? That is the reason that I like talking to people that I know are connected to God and are hearing Him; I need to know that the heaven is not closed over me.

In Malachi 3:10: **"Bring ye all the tithes into the storehouse, that there may be meat in mine house, and prove me now herewith, saith the LORD of hosts, if I will not open you the windows of heaven , and pour you out a blessing, that** *there shall* **not be room enough** *to receive it."* This is talking about the open heaven. Now if we are fulfilling all righteousness, we don't have to talk about tithing because we are already being obedient to that. Since we are, heaven is open over us and, therefore, we are walking under an open heaven. If we don't tithe, heaven is closed and we do not hear what everybody is hearing. When you are in a battle, you have to have an open heaven because we need clear instructions about what we should do at this particular point. We need to know what God is saying. I received a call from someone that reminded me that I said that they could call me whenever they needed an answer to questions. She left the message that a lady on her job insisted that she let her take care of her dogs and she lost one of them. She ended the call by requesting me to please call her back because she felt like she wanted to go over to the lady's house and hurt her. Now she is using scripture to find her dog. That is what Saul did to find his father's donkey; he went to see the Prophet. Now, unfortunately, her emotions are way up and she needs to know what to do because if she acts on her emotions, it will be the wrong thing. Many of us are listening to people who are under a closed heaven and we expect to win. Those that are doing that are not going to win because the people that they are listing to are not winning the battle. When you activate all four points, you will win every battle. The final point is:

4. **Receive the Spirit of God and walk in the light**. You have to walk in all the light that you know to walk in. Whatever revelation that you

have received from the word of God do that is the light you know.

Remember the reason that I am talking about this is because God told me, "I want you to prepare my people to exist on this battleground" Remember that there is an external and an internal battleground. The enemy never gets to your internal battle ground first. He comes onto your external battleground first in order to paralyze you and gain access to your internal, which is your thought realm. If he can paralyze you there, he can shut you down.

The reason we believe that he starts with our internal battleground is because we don't look at it as being a battle ground. We look at it from the perspective of a manifestation. By way of manifestation, he gets us to speak things that we would not ordinarily say. A famous person said this, "if the enemy within cannot hurt you, the enemy without can do you not harm". We give more attention to the enemy without and we are blind to the enemy within. The real enemy is in you. Say the word enemy very slowly—"En-e-my". If that can't hurt you, be confident that you will win every battle every time.

Review Questions:

1. What are two major reasons for our defeat in a battle?

2. What are the three things about the battleground you should know and understand?

3. What are the four principles Jesus used to position him to win every battle?

4. Name the two types of battles and their positions.

5. Name the levels of progression in the battlefield.

The Prophet and Deliverance

Chapter 8

Within the general makeup of the prophet, is the gift of discerning of spirits. This is or should be a gift that flows out of the prophetic person. The gift of discerning spirits along with the other eight gifts of the Spirit should be manifested in the life of the prophet, the prophetic minister, and occasionally those who function in prophetic gifting. It is the gift of discerning of spirits that will enable the prophet to supernaturally see the plans, purpose, and working of the enemy and its force. The gift of discerning of spirits will also give the prophet the ability to see into the realm of the spirit in order to clearly understand the maneuvering and the functioning of the spirit that is in operation and is giving physical manifestation at that time.

> "To another the working of miracles; to another prophecy, to another discerning of spirits; to another *divers* kinds of tongues; and to another the interpretation of tongues:"

I Corinthians 12:10

In **Mark 9:4-29**, a father brought his young boy who was possessed and had a physical manifestation of a deaf and dumb spirit to the Lord Jesus for deliverance. Let us take a look at some possible manifestations of a deaf and dumb spirit and how it would manifest itself at particular levels of oppression and possession. This example in Mark 9 is possession. But, this spirit may not always be in the form of possession. It may come in the form of oppression. Possession is the total control by a demonic force over an individual's soul (mind, will, emotion and intellect). Oppression is a force that would come against or attack the mind and/or the flesh. Oppression works from the outside. It is more emotional than spiritual.

It is the role and responsibility of the prophet to recognize and/or identify the various levels of spiritual and demonic influence within the congregation. It is important not to call what may be a work of the flesh demonic or what may be demonic a work of the flesh. We must identify what are the works of the flesh and not attempt to cast out what is not demonic.

The person operating in the works of the flesh is not necessarily demonic. **(Galatians 5:17-21)** The individual must take authority and control over their own flesh, bringing it into subjection to their recreated/born-again spirit. This begins the development of babes in Christ versus someone who continually walks in the flesh. The prophet would have to discern this area because of his authority to correct and/or chastise the body. Those that are babes will find themselves wrestling with their flesh. Once again, this does not mean that it is a demonic influence.

Recognizing Demonic Influence

We must be able to recognize the various stages of demonic influence. There are six stages:

1. **Regression** – Is to withdraw, or to back away from.

   We should be able to discern this stage within the midst of our congregation. People that begin to become isolated from the Body are in the stage of regression.

   When is this regression and when is this prophetic preparation? Regression does not allow you to interact with others. However, regressing prophetically will not prevent your interaction, but will cause conflict in forcing interaction because of your season.

2. **Suppression** – Is to keep from being revealed or to inhibit the expression of.

   It is manifested from lack of joy. A person begins to hide their feelings and is unable to express their joy. The prophet must be mindful of what he talks about or confesses. This is prophetic preparation. Suppression is different. Suppression is *denying* what they feel.

3. **Depression** – Is a broken spirit.

They are not able to overcome the things in their life. If not arrested, caught or put in check at this point, this will lead to oppression which opens the door to possession. Depression is a period of drastic decline. There is that time when the prophet goes into a desert place, but never a drastic decline.

4. **Oppression** – Is one who is weighted down with the cares of this world.

They lack victory. Oppression is to keep down by unjust use of authority or to weigh heavily on the mind or spirit. (**I Corinthians 7:37; 2 Corinthians 9:7 NIV or NASB**). The prophetic side of oppression is called discipline. Your flesh is being oppressed. Discipline is training expected to produce a specific character or pattern. School is the place of discipline and challenge.

5. **Obsession** – One who lacks reality

They become focused on one particular sin in their life. Obsession is a compulsive, often unreasonable idea or emotion; an irresistible impulse to act on an unreasonable idea, problem or thing. The quality should be on the prophet in a position sense. It should happen in a time of preparation.

6. **Possession** – Someone who comes under total control of a demonic force.

In our prophetic preparatory period we should come under the control of the Holy Spirit, which involves being totally submitted to Him. **(I Corinthians 16:14-16)** They have addicted themselves to the ministry of the saints.

The first five of these stages are mental and emotional harassment by the enemy. The sixth is spiritual, a total yielding of the person's soul to a demonic force. All of these stages, through the gift of discerning of spirits, can be discerned and the person can be delivered.

 **Review Questions:**

1. What is the gift of discerning of spirits?

2. What is the difference between oppression and possession?

3. Name in order the levels of demonic influence and define each one.

4. Is there a major difference in each level of influence? If so, how do they differ?

The Spirit of Perversion

Chapter 9

Perversion means to deviate from the original form or intent. People that are bound with this spirit make a choice to leave the natural use. Homosexuals are bound with the spirit of perversion. However, there are men that have never entered into a homosexual relationship that are bound by this spirit.

The Prophet's Role in Discernment

Through the prophet's spiritual insight, his/her ability to discern spiritual influence is great. Within the prophet's role and responsibilities in ministry, there will be times during impartation that it is necessary for him to be cognizant of various levels of demonic influence, oppression and/or possession. The prophet may from time-to- time, discern, cast out and/or deliver an individual from whatever level of demonic influence present.

130 | Foundations of Prophetic Maturity

Particular Spirits and How They Manifest

Mark 1:21-28 <u>A Religious Spirit</u> – The manifestation of this unclean spirit seemed to have a revelation of who Jesus was and a religious knowledge that would allow him to fit in with most religious people. **The remedy:** Jesus prophetically discerned the spirit, its function, and commanded him to hold his peace and come out of the man.

Mark 5:1-19 <u>A Spirit of Insanity</u> – The manifestation of this unclean spirit was able to tap into a portion of this man's mind and cause him to have incredible strength. This is a man that manifested multiple personalities through the influence of a demonic spirit that brought much damage to his body. But at a spare break from Demonic activity, he in the presence of Jesus, fell down and worshipped Him. This was a clear indication on the man's part that he wanted to be delivered.

The scriptures can help us identify the difference between a demonic spirit and a sickness. When Jesus was in the presence of sickness, there was not a spiritual or physical reaction. But when He was in the presence of demonic influence, there was a manifestation or a reaction within the person. Both physical and spiritual are present. The demonic spirit responds with a physical manifestation. The gift if discerning spirits is one of the many gifts within the Body of Christ. *"Now ye are the body of Christ and members in particular."*

 **Review Questions:**

1. Define perversion.

2. What are some of the behaviors of someone influenced by a religious spirit?

3. What are some of the behaviors of someone influence by a spirit of insanity?

4. Is there a difference between the presence of a demonic spirit and sickness? If so, how does a prophet discern what is in operation?

Identifying Prophetic Manifestations in You

Chapter 10

Jurisdiction Realm:

The levels of jurisdiction, influence and expertise of the prophetic arm

The Prophet to the Nations

This prophet has the ability to see into the nations that have been assigned to him. This prophet has a word to nations and kingdoms. In addition, he or she has several realms of authority:

- National and international authority

- National and international insights

- National and international sensitivity to seasons and times

- National and international dominion over kingdoms and nations

It is important that as we discuss the prophet types we know where we fall individually. Once we identify exactly where we are in the prophetic, we will come to understand our realm of authority. If we understand where we fit in the prophetic scheme of things, we will receive an increase of the anointing on our lives, an understanding of how we operate, and a place to focus our attention so that we don't wander around within the prophetic or apostolic, not knowing where we fit.

This prophet type's realm of authority transcends regional boundaries. The prophet to the nations differs from a regional prophet. A regional prophet has only regional authority. In contrast, the prophet to the nations has ruling authority in nations, kingdoms, *and* regions. This prophet cannot be limited. It is also worth noting that this prophet has a relationship with God and knows that he or she needs to be sensitive to the Holy Spirit in order to carry out his or her assignment.

A prime example of the prophet to the nations is found in the Book of Jeremiah:

> *"Then the word of the Lord came unto me, saying, Before I formed thee in the belly I knew thee; and before thou*

camest forth out of the womb I sanctified thee, and I ordained thee a prophet unto the nations. Then said I,

Ah, Lord GOD!, behold, I cannot speak; for I am a child. But the LORD said unto me, Say not, I am a child: for thou shalt go to all that I shall send thee, and whatsoever I command thee thou shalt speak. Be not afraid of their faces: for I am with thee to deliver thee, saith the LORD. Then the LORD put forth his hand, and touched my mouth. And the LORD said unto me, Behold, I have put my words in thy mouth. See, I have this day set thee over the nations and over the kingdoms, to root out, and to pull down, and to destroy, and to throw down, to build, and to plant. Moreover the word of the LORD came unto me, saying, Jeremiah, what seest thou? And I said, I see a rod of an almond tree. Then said the LORD unto me, Thou hast well seen: for I will hasten my word to perform it."

Jeremiah 1:4-12

In verses 4 and 5, God specifically called Jeremiah to be a prophet to the nations: **"Then the word of the LORD came unto me, saying, Before I formed thee in the belly I knew thee; and before thou camest forth out of the womb I sanctified thee, *and* I ordained thee a prophet unto the nations."** Because of this, do not take it for granted when God begins to speak to you and it seems that He speaks to you regarding only a particular area or nation.

 **Key Point:**

As a prophet, you have to be able to fit into several categories and venues. You cannot just look like what you came from. As a prophet to the nations, you have to forget about where you came from and concentrate on what God has called you to reach.

In addition, we need to understand that God is not just speaking to this prophet type regarding a particular group and then not wanting him or her to be associated with that group in any way.

Let's say, for instance, that God profoundly speaks to you about the Charismatic Church. He doesn't deal with you regarding the Baptist, the Pentecostal, the African Methodist Episcopal, the Christian Methodist Episcopal, or the United Methodist Episcopal Churches. Yet, you are a part of the Church of God in Christ (COGIC). Somewhere and somehow, you are not going to be totally associated with the COGIC because it seems as if you are a prophet to the Charismatic Church. It seems this way because the only thing that God is talking to you about is the Charismatic

Church. God has given you vision for what the Charismatic Church is to do. Therefore, you will have some interaction—probably on a high level—with the Charismatic Church. If, however, you look as though you are a "carbon copy"

of the Church of God in Christ, the Charismatic Church to which God has assigned you will reject you. In other words, you can't look like *that* if you're called to *this.*

"Then said I, Ah, LORD God, behold, I cannot speak: for I am a child. But the LORD said unto me, Say not, I am a child: for thou shalt go to all that I shall send thee, and whatsoever I command thee thou shalt speak."
Jeremiah 1:6-7

The apostle Paul deals with this in **Philippians 3:4-8**

"Though I might also have confidence in the flesh. If any other man thinketh that he hath whereof he might trust in the flesh, I more: Circumcised the eighth day, of the stock of Israel, *of* the tribe of Benjamin, a Hebrew of the Hebrews; as touching the law, a Pharisee; Concerning zeal, persecuting

the church; touching the righteousness which is in the law, blameless. But what things were gain to me, those I counted loss for Christ. Yea doubtless, and I count all things *but* loss for the excellency of the knowledge of Christ Jesus my Lord: for whom I have suffered the loss of all things, and do count them *but* dung, that I may win Christ,..."

And in **1 Corinthians 2:1-2:**

"And I, brethren, when I came to you, came not with excellency of speech or of wisdom, declaring unto you the testimony of God. For I determined not to know any thing among you, save Jesus Christ, and him crucified."

And, finally, again in **1 Corinthians 9:19-22**

"For though I be free from all *men*, yet have I made myself servant unto all, that I might gain the more. And unto the Jews I became as a Jew, that I might gain the Jews; to them that are under the law, as under the law, that I might gain them that are under the law; To them that are without law, as without law, (being not without law to God, but under the law to Christ,) that I might gain them that are without law. To the

weak became I as weak, that I might gain
the weak: I am made all things to all *men*,
that I might by all means save some."

It is also important to note that, as you go into
particular kingdoms, nations and regions, you will
notice the differences in peoples' faces. This is why you
can never be moved by the faces of people (**Jeremiah
1:8**), but you must be able to int them.

As a prophet to the nations, you must be able to
interpret. This is where we must clean up ourselves. If
we are dealing with things according to our hang-ups,
we will misinterpret the message. For example, I look at
someone's face, interpret the message through my
hang-ups and arrive at the conclusion that, "Oh, he's
mad at me." In actuality, he hasn't even given me a
second thought. I arrived at the assumption that he was
angry with me because I misinterpreted the message.

God told Jeremiah not to be moved by their faces.
Likewise, as a prophet to the nations, you cannot be
affected by what's on a person's face; nor should you
treat or mistreat someone based on what's on his or her
face. We should love everyone. When you put loving
everyone into practice, you will be able to handle people

with care in spite of what your head is telling you. Because their faces do not move you, you can show them the love of God and speak into their lives without bitter thoughts. This is totally important for the prophet to the nations.

"Then the Lord put forth his hand,
and touched my mouth. And the
LORD said unto me, Behold, I have put
my words in thy mouth. See, I have
this day set thee over the nations and
over the kingdoms, to root out, and to
pull down, and to destroy and to
throw down, to build, and to plant."
Jeremiah 1:9-10

Whatever God Touches Is Anointed

God touches the prophet's mouth to command him to speak exactly what He has told him to speak. On the other hand, the rooting out, pulling down, destroying, throwing down, building, and planting will take some level of correctly judging or discerning that particular nation or that particular individual so that you will clearly understand what God wants them to do.

When we say that we will judge a nation or an individual, it simply means that we will closely examine their faults and strengths. This thorough examination will allow us to know how to compensate for the faults. All of this is done in an effort to determine what God has actually called this particular nation or individual to do so that we, the prophet to the nations, can know what to effectively speak into that nation or individual causing God's desire to come to pass. Once we understand what a nation, individual, church, or region is

called to do, then we can judge it. As a prophet to the nations, it becomes our responsibility, to make up for the faults or to compensate. We are the ones who will have to pray it in.

When we see the condition of someone's situation, what do we REALLY think about it? When God saw that the earth was empty, void, without form and dark—what did God REALLY think about it? God thought about what He needed to make of it because of what it was not. He saw darkness and created light. He saw water and spoke lands into existence. God knew that once He placed land in the earth that water would be needed. So, God divided the waters from the waters. God figured all of this out in advance. He wasn't moved by the fact that everything was

 **Key Point:**

Most problems are really someone's answers—they're just answers that are out of place. Being out of place makes the answers *look* like problems.

flooded out. He didn't view the flooding as a problem. God looked at it as a solution. Therefore, He repositioned the solution. But, we do the opposite. We look at the problem as a problem as opposed to looking at the problem as a solution.

Examples of Prophets to the Nation

Elisha

Elijah observed Elisha doing a wonderful job of shepherding oxen for his father. At this point, God had already spoken to him, but Elisha had one of the worst positions anyone could have—walking behind someone's oxen. But, Elisha followed the oxen well. Let's reposition this tremendous problem of following oxen and following in what the oxen periodically release—waste.

Elisha, considering all of this, continued to follow behind the oxen. He didn't become discouraged because he stepped in a lot of dung in his bare feet. No! He kept on going, ensuring that he took good care of his father's oxen. God saw his tenacity and care and repositioned him. Elisha ceased from walking behind the oxen and was repositioned to the front side of his people.

Elisha's walking behind the oxen looked like a problem; but he became someone's solution. Elisha answered someone's questions. It is important to note that you have to learn how to walk behind before you can walk up front and answer someone's questions.

We don't walk behind a particular person or persons for no reason at all. We walk behind long enough to become an influence. Because of this, when God repositions us up front, the people can see the advantage of following.

The Prophet to the Nations must know that God Himself set him/her over nations and kingdoms **(Jeremiah 1:10)**. This prophet type, as stated earlier, has authority over nations and kingdoms. He or she must also be sensitive to the Holy Spirit. This prophet is able to be in one region and be sensitive to something that is going on in another region. This prophet type

must understand seasons and times and know what the particular nation; kingdom and region are designed to do in order to speak a word that brings forth manifestation.

In **Jeremiah 1:11-12**, we find that the prophet to the nations is anointed to see what is in his realm of authority and experiences the "fine tuning" of God. God doesn't play with what He says. Whatever it is that He says He will begin to bring to pass. In other words, He will hasten His word to perform it.

Ezekiel

Another Prophet to the Nations is Ezekiel.

"And he said unto me, Son of man, stand upon thy feet, and I will speak unto thee. And the spirit entered into me when he spake unto me, and set me upon my feet, that I heard him that spake unto me. And he said unto me, Son of man, I send thee to the children of Israel, to a rebellious nation that hath rebelled against me: they and their fathers have transgressed against me, even unto this very day."
Ezekiel 2:1-3

One of the first things that we must see in this passage of scripture is that God commanded Ezekiel to stand upon his feet before He began speaking to him. Contrary to what we have often believed, you are not always going to be on your face when God speaks. Most of us are too religious; so we wait on a particular religious order or move to take place before God speaks. God will speak at any given time.

This prophet to the nations, Ezekiel, was sent to a specific nation of people, the nation of Israel, and received specific information for them. When we really grasp this concept, we will stop minding other folks' business. God is not talking to you about *them*; He is talking to you about you. God is not talking to you, a prophet to the nations, about someone else's nation; He's only talking to you about **your** nation. One of the things that we always want to do is to find out what the Lord is saying about *them.*

You will not find one time when Jesus asked God to speak to Him—not one. Jesus understood

that if He held His position with God in an intimate way that God would automatically say something to Him if He wanted to communicate the information. If God didn't want to communicate information, then it was none of Jesus' business. This statement is proven in Matthew 24, when Jesus spoke these words to His disciples regarding the end times:

Verily I say unto you, This generation shall not pass, till all

 **Key Point:**

Prophets, by nature, are nosey. When we have insight, we don't place boundaries around it. Because we fail to do so, we become nosey. As prophets to the nations, we must guard ourselves from nosiness and becoming busybodies.

these things be fulfilled. Heaven and
earth shall pass away, but my words
shall not pass away. But of that day
and hour knoweth no man, no, not the
angels of heaven, but my Father only.
Matthew 24:34-36.

Regional Prophets and Prophets to the Nations stay within the boundaries of their information and understand those boundaries. In addition, they reject persons who try to convince them to wander outside of the boundaries of their information. They do this because they already understand, from the Lord, what their turf is. The regional prophet, who we will discuss later, understands that he or she has nothing to do with the nations. And, the Prophet to the Nations understands his or her realm of authority.

The prophet Ezekiel was sent to a rebellious nation. Rebellion, being *"as the sin of witchcraft,"* allows us to know what the nation was involved in. They were in rebellion so why didn't God just wipe out the whole rebellious nation of Israel to find another nation? The nation of Israel had a word from God!

I say then, Hath God cast away his
people? God forbid. For I also am an
Israelite, of the seed of Abraham, of the

*tribe of Benjamin. God hath not cast
away his people which he foreknew..."*
Romans 11:1-2a

God would not have given a prophet to this nation if
He had not intended to correct it (Israel). That is what
God was actually after—correcting the nation. God
didn't see it as a problem. God saw a man from the
nation becoming the solution for that nation.

Another reason that God did not cast the nation of
Israel away was that He needed to keep an Israelite on
the scene in order to be able to get Israel healed. When
the Jews become ready for total healing and a great
influx of Jews come into the kingdom, God's got to wake
up some Jews again. It's not going to be "we" who will
evangelize to them; it will be one of their own.

Isn't it amazing that God always leaves a remnant?
That remnant is important for the Hebrews. And that
savior, Moses, said to the creator, "You cannot destroy
them, lest those that are not of this class of people say
that the reason you destroyed the people was that you
couldn't bring them out." God, then, repented or
changed His mind.

One of the assignments of the prophet was to turn the
heart of the fathers to the children and the heart of the
children to their fathers **(Malachi 4:6)**. It is your
responsibility as a Prophet to the Nations, to turn the

heart of that child back to that father so that God can heal that child. As a result of the child's healing, the child will—in turn—reach the nation and bring about healing.

The most difficult crime to solve is an "inside job." This is a principle. Don't you think that God has enough sense to know that if He gets someone inside to solve it, then it becomes difficult for the Devil to attack him or her because he can't locate them? God got them from the *inside*. If God had chosen someone from the outside, it would have been easy to identify him or her.

Adopting this principle is utterly impossible. For example; if you are a woman who was totally messed up by a man, it is utterly impossible for a woman to heal you? Likewise, if you are a man who was totally messed up by a woman, it is utterly impossible for a man to heal you? The healing will come from no one other than the kind that hurt you.

 **Key Point:**

If a man is going to be healed, he will be healed by the kind that messed him up. The prophet to the nations must be conscious of the multifaceted responsibility assigned to him or her. Failing to do so could rob nations, kingdoms, or individuals of their healing.

The principle of this statement is found in **Ezekiel 22:30:**

> **"And I sought for a man among them, that should make up the hedge, and stand in the gap before me**

for the land, that I should not destroy it: but I found none."

Healing has to come from someone who is among the people. Every time a nation got into trouble, God sought for a man among them—not from among some other group. God is not going to reach all the way to Africa to heal America. If America is to be healed, she will be healed by her own kind. God is not going to allow America to go over to Africa and heal Africa. If Africa is going to be healed, she, too, will be healed by her own kind—by an African.

The In-House Prophet

This prophet is assigned to the house or local church. At the discretion of the set gift, he/she may give a word to the set gift, to the congregation, or to an individual. The in-house prophet, conversely, has "in-house" jurisdiction. His jurisdiction does not venture beyond his own house. This prophet type is responsible for ensuring that the information he receives gets to the one to whom he is submitted—in the house. If this person has been released as an in-house prophet, then, by all means, this prophet has the ability to dispense the information he received throughout the body over which he has been given authority.

As long as the in-house prophet has been released, he or she has in-house authority, which includes the release to prophesy and to interpret messages that have been given in tongues.

The Regional Prophet

This prophet is assigned to a particular region and is responsible for prophesying into that region. The regional prophet is responsible for giving information to all of those who are in his or her particular region.

The Regional Prophet will hear what particular churches need to understand in the house. They will also hear information regarding their region. This may prove to be a sticky area for this prophet type. The Regional Prophet must come to understand that the word he receives <u>may be a word for his region, but not necessarily for his church</u>. In other words, he must decipher the word he receives to be either a *general word* or a *direct word*. What is the difference between the two?

A direct word is tailored for me specifically. If a direct word comes specifically for me, that is my word. No one else can use that word and the one who works that word will be the one who will have fulfilled prophecy after that word. Being anointed and saved does not guarantee that the word someone prophesied to you will come to pass.

In like manner, if the word that was prophesied to you does not come to pass, that doesn't mean that the person who gave you that word is a false prophet. It just means that you didn't work the word.

Some prophecy is conditional. Most of us remember the word that the prophet Isaiah gave to Hezekiah as recorded in **Isaiah 38:1, "...Thus saith the LORD, Set thine house in order: for thou shalt die, and not live."** This was a prophecy that did not come to pass in the time that it was to be fulfilled. Now, Hezekiah did eventually die, but the prophecy that was given to him by Isaiah was conditional.

As we will discuss in detail later, there is a difference between a *"word of wisdom"* and a *"word of prophecy."* Although they look like alike, they are quite different. A word of wisdom cannot be changed or altered. It is an event that is already scheduled in time. It is an event that is coming. A word of prophecy, however, may be conditional. We can see this in Hezekiah's response to the word that the prophet Isaiah gave him:

"Then Hezekiah turned his face toward the wall, and prayed unto the LORD, And said, Remember now, O LORD, I beseech thee, how I have walked before thee in truth and with a perfect heart, and have done that which is good in thy sight. And Hezekiah wept sore."
Isaiah 38:2-3

In other words, Hezekiah cried out to God on his own behalf. God responded, in turn, by saying to Isaiah in the fifth verse, **"Go, and say to Hezekiah, Thus saith the LORD, the God of David thy father, I have heard thy prayer, I have seen thy tears: behold, I will add unto thy days fifteen years."** God added fifteen years to Hezekiah's life when Hezekiah was scheduled to die. By doing what he was supposed to do, Hezekiah was given fifteen years—on credit—to live and to get his house in order.

From Hezekiah's near-death experience, we find that prophecy was altered for a period of time simply because of the grace and mercy of God. Hezekiah pleaded his case before God and God granted him mercy. The prophecy, as it turns out, was conditional.

 **Review Questions:**

1. What is the difference between "word of wisdom" and "word of prophecy"?

2. What is the difference between a "general word" and a "direct word"?

3. What are the realms of authority a prophet to nations would be assigned?

4. How does the jurisdictional authority for the In-House Prophet differ from that of a Regional Prophet?

5. Which type of prophet has ruling authority in nations, kingdoms and regions?

ABOUT THE AUTHOR

"Jeremiah 1:9-10 (KJV) ⁹ Then the LORD put forth his hand, and touched my mouth. And the LORD said unto me, Behold, I have put my words in thy mouth. ¹⁰ See, I have this day set thee over the nations and over the kingdoms, to root out, and to pull down, and to destroy, and to throw down, to build, and to plant.

Bishop Rodney S. Walker I is a dynamic prophetic voice whose ministry is renowned as being a catalytic agent for understanding and maturing in the prophetic.

A native of Washington, D.C., Bishop Walker is the Founder and Senior Pastor of Heritage Church International, established in 1990 in Waldorf, Maryland. He serves as the General Overseer of Bishop R. S. Walker Ministries - formerly Another Touch of Glory Ministries - that covers national and international churches, para-church ministries and businesses.

He is spiritually covered by and accountable to Dr. Michael Freeman of Spirit of Faith Christian Center in Temple Hills, Maryland. He is also submitted to his Spiritual Father, Bishop Ralph L. Dennis of Kingdom Fellowship Covenant Ministries in Towson, Maryland.

In addition to being a graduate of the Jericho Christian Training College, Bishop R.S.Walker received his Doctor of Divinity degree from The Spirit of Truth Institute. Bishop R. S. Walker's training by versatile and equipped instructors, guidance from his Mentor, as well as submission to his Spiritual Father, has developed him into a well-balanced, grounded, and seasoned prophet.

In 1999, Bishop Walker founded the School of the Prophets. The School has locations in Waldorf and Baltimore, MD, Raleigh and Wilson, NC, Abuja, Nigeria, York, Pa, and has been hosted throughout the United States and beyond using online streaming.

In addition to equipping and training in the prophetic, Bishop Walker has also assembled a body of Prophetic Presbyters who assist him in managing the great assignment God has set to his hands.

Bishop Walker is the author and publisher of over 10 books including: *The Prophetic Prayer Journal, Raising Prophets of Character, Becoming a Proven Prophetic Voice, The 21st Century Prophet, The Renaissance Prophet, and The Father/Son Encounter* all of which prove to be phenomenal resources of the serious believer's library.

Among Bishop Walker's many accomplishments, is that of being a devoted husband to his lovely wife, Pastor Betty Walker, and a loving father to his eleven wonderful children.

Bishop Rodney S. Walker's ultimate goal is to fulfill all that God has purposed for his life and to effectively lead those placed in his prophetic and pastoral care. His love for God is evident in his preaching, teaching and zeal for ministry. You will experience the wind of the Spirit through this Man of God.

Order Form

Bishop RS Walker Ministries

2760 Crain Highway
Waldorf, MD 20601
301- 843-9267 or 877-200-8967
Fax 240-585-7073
www.bishoprswalkerproducts.com
e-mail: admin@bishoprswalker.com

Name	
Title	
Date	
Church/Ministry	
Address	
City	State
Zip	
Daytime Phone	E-mail

Items Ordered:

Description	CD	DVD	Book	Qty	Total
Raising Prophets of Character Book			$14.95		
School of the Prophets 15-week Course	$190.00			Disc	$110.00
School of the Prophets Live Training					$250.00
School of Prophetic Intercession					$200.00
Prophetic Dominion Series	$34.00	$47.00			
Renaissance Prophet's Manual			$33.95		
The Art of Tongues Book			$ 9.99		
Raising Prophets of Character Prayer Devotional			$14.99		
Creating Habits for a Functional Life			$14.99		
The Father Son Encounter			$16.95		
The Fundamentals of Faith (6-CDs)	$50.00				

Power of First Fruit Offerings (6-CDs) $30.00 $60.00

Shipping Information:	Total price of items
Add $5 for Priority Mail for first item and $1 per each additional item MD add 6% sales tax	Add shipping charge
	Tax (if applicable)
	Total Amount Enclosed

Method of Payment:

Please charge my: Discover   MasterCard   VISA   AMEX

Card Number: Expiration Date (Month/Year):

☐☐☐☐☐☐☐☐☐☐☐☐☐   ☐☐☐☐

Signature (as shown on credit card):

Check or Money Order
(made payable to Bishop RS Walker Ministries)

For Speaking Engagements contact:

Office of the Bishop Administrative
Staff Phone: 301-843-9267
Fax: 240-585-7093

Made in the USA
Charleston, SC
13 April 2015